"*Grace Changes Everything* is a [...] desperately needed today. In th[...] the deception of a performanc[...] adventure of living a life fully immersed in the grace God offers us moment by moment. If you are tired, frustrated and discouraged, there is incredible hope. Grace really does change everything."

Drew Stephens, pastor of the International Church of Prague, Czech Republic

"*Grace Changes Everything* is an accessible and beautifully written testimony and teaching on God's love, the identity He has given us in Christ, and how we can live life freely in the grace He gives. Janna's words will have you laughing, crying, reflecting, repenting, and ultimately, with open hands, receiving the grace and love that the Father lavishly pours out on His children. With vulnerability and candidness, she reveals her own struggle with a Performance Driven Life and God's work to gently guide her toward a grace-centered life. I am convinced that the women of the church today, including myself, desperately need to hear Janna's words and message that ultimately point us to God's love—that astounding, ineffable, lavish, scandalous, enormous, unchanging, grand, steady, and furious LOVE."

Davina Perret, director of Woman's Ministries, Deer Creek Church, Littleton, CO

"As someone who is a 'doer' and has struggled with grace on the other side of defeat, the soothing words of this book were a beautiful reminder of God's unconditional love and unmerited favor. *Grace Changes Everything* is a poetic must read for those struggling to grasp the depth of His grace or looking for a reminder that His sacrifice covers not only the moment of salvation but outflows as a sweet gift into our everyday lives."

Brittany Rust, author, speaker, and pastor at Red Rocks Church

"Janna Wright brings a witty yet forthright approach to a familiar crisis in the lives of many Christian women—a guilt-driven approach to serving. Readers will journey with her into the refreshing freedom of a life lived in the abundance of God's grace and discover for themselves that 'grace is enough!' Don't miss out on the adventure that can also become your very own!"

Linda Lesniewski, women's minister of Green Acres Baptist Church, Tyler, Texas, & author of *Women at the Cross* and *Connecting Women: A Guide for Leaders in Women's Ministry*

"*Grace Changes Everything* offers good news for 'good' Christians who are burning themselves out through (sometimes unconscious) standards of perfection. With humor and dead-eye accuracy, author Janna Wright reveals astonishing vulnerability as she testifies to the love of God that transforms imperfect people, which is to say all of us. What a relief to read a self-help book that focuses not on doing, but on being!"

Louise Westfall, pastor of Central Presbyterian Church

"While reading Janna's words and feeling her heart, I felt that I was reading my own personal journal entries. Janna opened my eyes to a Christian reality of being a busy servant in the church. Her words have given me a new appreciation of God's Grace in being "busy" in ministry."

Sherri Moore, former Women's Ministry Director,
Pikes Peak Christian Church, Colorado Springs, CO

"Sometimes you bump into God so hard that it hurts. It also gets your attention. When God shows us truths in ourselves we are often tempted to run from them, deny them or justify them. If only we'd stop talking at God long enough to absorb the love behind the truth He's shown us. That Love—that Grace—it transforms us. And out of that transformation may come the very thing we tried so hard to do in our own strength, but never could have achieved. We just might help someone else bump into Jesus."

Lisa Steven, Executive Director, Hope House of Colorado

"Janna beautifully writes for every woman who struggles with an identity of being 'enough.' A life lived in Christ is supposed to be a life of abundance—not a tasteless, 'cardboard' kind of life. But what does that mean? *Grace Changes Everything* compels us to look—really seek out—our Father and find our 'enough-ness' in the center of His defining love that He has for us."

Wendy Holden, Equipping Director of Women
and Senior Adults, Foothills Bible Church

"While the world may exhaust us with an unrelenting list of needs and demands, our Father has something better! The conversational tone and humor of *Grace Changes Everything* allows the reader to take a deep breath and cozy on in. This book is a beautiful reminder of how God sees us through a lens of love and unending grace."

Gabrielle Oldfield, Women's Ministry Coordinator,
Jubilee Fellowship Church (Highlands Ranch Campus)

Grace CHANGES Everything

HOW TO BE ENOUGH IN A DO-MORE WORLD

BY

{ JANNA WRIGHT }

To the women who serve tirelessly in ministry . . .
You deserve a dozen thank-yous,
a dazzling vacation,
and a great big grace hug.

Contents

Introduction

"What do you do?"

"Um, I'm an SAHN," I'd mumble.

"Oh, really? What's that?"

"A stay-at-home nothing. I have no job right now and zero kids. I clean the house sometimes and cook dinner most nights, but I . . . well . . . um, you know."

Then I'd smile apologetically.

* * *

I once loathed being asked what I do. I suppose the question is to be expected when you move across the country and don't know a soul in your new town. We were visiting churches, looking for new friends and community, so it made sense that I heard this "unofficial American greeting" often. But why the loathing?

Maybe I'd heard it so often it sounded tinny, like the "Fifteen minutes could save you" commercial or the radio song you roll your eyes at after having heard it for the twentieth time. Or maybe it was that when someone would ask me, "Who are you and what do you do?" my cheeks would start to burn and I'd bite my lip. How do you answer that question when you don't *do* anything?

Most people are desensitized to the unofficial American greeting. Anymore, it's just a social nicety we expect. We're programmed to answer with short, clear phrases:

"I'm Jodi, home health care nurse."
"Katherine, divorced mom of one."
"It's Emily, blogger and church volunteer."

For most of my life the answer was easy for me too:

"I'm Janna, oldest of seven."
"I'm Janna, graduate student majoring in fine arts."
"I'm Janna, Christian school teacher."
"I'm Janna, new wife."
"I'm Janna, church music leader."

These post-comma words give us a feeling of security. They let us categorize an identity quickly and easily: "This is me in a nutshell."

These short answers are never the whole story, though, are they? We are far more complex characters than a simple job, label, or role can encompass. We've held too many positions, worn too many hats, and lived too much life to be reduced to a single post-comma phrase. Besides, what happens when life takes a turn and the answer changes?

After I moved more than seventeen hundred miles across the country and realized I didn't have a good answer anymore, it left me all uncomfortable and out of sorts. Hence, the loathing. I resented the who-are-you-what-do-you-do question. For a while I stumbled over my tongue or tried to deflect. I even boycotted for a bit, which was not pretty, let me tell you! I hoped that eventually I'd come up with a witty, mildly snarky reply that would satisfy people and make me feel better. I figured that would be the end of it.

But, boy was I wrong. What happened next was *much* worse.

In a moment, my entire life, belief system, and what was left of my poor, little identity shattered into pieces around me. How would I ever find post-comma words again?

We're all searching for post-comma words. Whether we realize it or not, it's a life mission. As humans we long, no, *need* to know who we are so we can make sense of the world. So we understand ourselves. So we know what to do. So we are confident that our lives matter somewhere, somehow.

That is one of the main reasons for this book: to share the story of how my labels were rewritten. I want to empathize in this drama we all face, this search for knowing. And I long to speak out against the misnomers we've endured, adopted, or have had handed to us.

See, when I came face-to-face with my post-comma drama, I was shocked at how much I hated what I saw. I've faced the "not sure," "don't know," and "kinda hate it" answers, and I've been surprised to find a life-changing journey just beyond the comma—a journey into knowing who I truly am and not just what people assume, society claims, or labels state about me.

I also write because I have a secret wish: that you too are ready for the journey of a lifetime. This search for the best and truest post-comma words is *about* your very lifetime!

So, my brave co-journeyer, thank you for opening this book, feasting on its pages, and being willing to take a few steps into my story. It's not always pretty. Some of it may appall you, make you laugh out loud, or break your heart. I know it has me.

*SPOILER ALERT: There's a happy ending, as much as this monumental life season can be called an "ending" anyway. It's really more like a beginning, I guess, as so many of the big, God-moments of our lives are. You and I are just amazing stories after all, with oh-so-many scene changes, unexpected characters, and plot twists no one ever saw coming.

That's probably the best way to describe this: as the biggest plot twist I never saw coming, a crazy, wild ride that begins "Janna, Stellar Performer" and ends . . . well, walk with me there and see.

{1}

Do You Hear What I Hear?

I hear voices.

These voices chatter in my head so much I hardly even realize they're there. What do they say? Most of the time they tell me stories about how I'm doing or who I am at the moment.

Like one morning while watching TV during breakfast, a voice in my head wondered, *Do you think that diet pill actually works? Most of those are a hoax, right?*

Of course they are! What are you thinking?! countered my rational head voice. He's always quick to point out how culture emphasizes beauty and an attractive body, and it's his self-appointed job to shield me from societal influence. But sometimes the other voices sneak through despite his best efforts.

But what if this pill's for real? Seems like an easy way to lose a little weight. Not much work involved. No crazy diet. Just take a horse pill every morning, and voila! Wouldn't you be happier if you slimmed down a couple sizes, hmm?

Soon another voice piped in, *Let's get this kitchen whipped into shape! Just wash that last frying pan, wipe those counters, and you're done with the breakfast dishes. Wait, it's not even eight yet? Look who's rocking her day already!* And I stood a little taller and nodded my head with satisfaction as I remembered sermons about being a good steward of your God-given resources like time and money.

Then there was the time I woke up with such a foggy head I toyed with skipping breakfast altogether—until an internal voice cautioned, *If you really loved your husband, you'd make him breakfast this morning. It doesn't have to be anything fancy like bacon, but he sure appreciates it when you cook his eggs. That's what a good wife would do.*

I sighed wistfully. I really *want* to be a good wife. I grew up with a fabulous role model, not to mention the "good helpmeet" expectations Christianity instilled in me.

So I listened to the voice and made breakfast, even though it meant I cracked the eggs a little harder than necessary and threw the pans into the sink a little more loudly than usual.

So, yeah, I hear voices often.

Funny thing is, you hear them too—your own head voices, I mean. Oh, yours may not sound exactly like mine, but yours tell you stories about who you are and how you're doing too.

Want to test the theory?

Close your eyes for twenty seconds and concentrate on your

thoughts. What story are you hearing right now?

I feel silly.
This is weird.
Is anybody looking at me?
Why in the world is she asking me to do this crazy thing?

Now think back to when you woke up this morning. What was your first thought when you opened your eyes or put on your gym shoes or shuffled to get coffee? What story did you hear about what you needed to do or who you are?

Busy day!
Three appointments on the calendar.
Overslept again. *Late already.*
Good mom. Lousy wife. Overcommitted. Tired.
Excited because today's my birthday . . . .

Sounds like a case of head voices to me! But not to worry. It's not magic, early-onset psychosis or something to mention to your therapist. It's the way you and I were designed. God created us to think in story, and we hear and tell ourselves stories all the time: stories about how we're doing, about what things mean, and about who we are.

These stories are often formed with the help of the external voices of culture, family, and religion. In fact, some of those voices in your head may remind you of people you know: a parent, pastor, coach, spouse, colleague, or friend. That's because we accumulate our stories from a variety of sources.

The Twin Terrors

A special pair of voices also plagues us. They piggyback on the culture, family, and religion stories—almost as enforcers, if you will. The Twin Terrors remind me of Dr. Seuss's Thing 1 and Thing 2, but instead of smiling faces and cute, blue unitards, these guys act more like Voldemort's long-lost cousins.

The Twin Terrors wear bright football jerseys. Thing 1 wears a puke-green jersey with his name embroidered on the back in large letters, "GUILT." On his chest is a circle monogram with the simple word, "DO." Guilt is the voice that keeps tabs on your behavior. It's his self-appointed job to gleefully let you know how well you're doing, especially if the answer is "not great."

- *I can't believe you didn't check your calendar so you missed that appointment!*
- *Did you see her house? Yours could look that way if you actually picked up a dust mop now and then.*
- *You botched that proposal. See, you should've prepared better.*
- *Dinner wasn't very good tonight. You really should try cooking more of those recipes you pin.*
- *You ought to exercise more.*
- *You shouldn't stay up so late writing blog posts.*

Guilt rarely travels alone. He prefers to team up with his twin. Thing 2 wears a bright jersey too, but it's fiery red. His sports the name "SHAME" across the back, and monogrammed on the front is his focus word, "BE." While Guilt focuses on what you do, Shame tells you who you are—and it's never pretty where Shame is concerned.

Guilt: You missed that appointment.
Shame: You are a disorganized disgrace.

Guilt: You botched the proposal.
Shame: You are a failure.

Guilt: You didn't cook a very good meal.
Shame: You are not a good wife.

Guilt: You should exercise more.
Shame: You are irresponsible.

Guilt: You shouldn't stay up so late writing blog posts.
Shame: You are a lousy planner.

Guilt and Shame terrorize people everywhere and especially thrive within families. I don't know if it's that we know how to push each other's buttons, that there are so many expectations, or that we just know each other so well we think we have the right to judge. Whatever the reason, Guilt and Shame use family relationships as a personal playground.

I'm the oldest in a family of seven children: five boys and two girls. Growing up, we siblings were pretty close, which delighted my mom. One thing Mom used to tell me was, "Janna, when I'm dead and gone, it's up to you to keep the family together."

Please understand my mom is alive and well and on track for a fully tenured professor position at the college where she teaches. A few years ago she began running half marathons and can still outlast me on all-day shopping trips. She is pretty much as Puerto Rican perky as ever! That was just her way of telling me close family relationships are important to her.

But Guilt loves to throw this line at me, especially with all seven of us kids grown, starting families of our own, and settling in various spots around the country. Guilt takes me down a well-traveled road with potholes like, *You won't be able to keep your family connected like your mom hoped. It's too hard because everyone lives far apart. Besides, you never keep up with your siblings like you should.* I ride with him in that stuffy car until Shame chimes in with his own chorus of, *See, you're not a good sister or a good daughter.*

Hello, Twin Terrors. It hurts to travel your all-too familiar road again.

Is Some Guilt Good?

For many of us, guilt trips are an expected way of life. Guilt is an easy way to keep behavior in line, and there comes a point where we've taken the trips so often it doesn't surprise us to pack the bags anymore.

Maybe you're thinking, *Yeah, but what about God? Doesn't He use guilt to bring us to repentance? Isn't some guilt good?*

Great question! If we were never introduced to God's law and how we've fallen short, we could not realize our need for a Savior. We deserve condemnation for our sin, and guilt over breaking God's law is necessary to bring us to repentance.

The key, though, is the *intent* behind the guilt. Before salvation, guilt helps you understand you are a sinner, unable to measure up to God's holy standard. That guilt draws you to accept Jesus and His forgiveness. Now, if you sin as a believer, the Holy Spirit nudges you to repent, you confess, and God instantly forgives.

But, think about the stories Guilt throws at you most often in the Christian life. Aren't the guilt stories usually condemning you for things you could've done better? Or good things you should've done but didn't? That kind of guilt is counterfeit. Counterfeit guilt masquerades itself in a couple of ways:

1. *Failure Reminder.* God never uses guilt to reinforce our past failures. He will not hound us with guilt over something that's already been confessed. So, if you continue to feel guilty about a sin you've already dealt with in the past, whether long ago or recently, that guilt is a counterfeit! (See Romans 8:1.)

2. *Performance Enhancer.* God never uses guilt to make us perform well. His methods involve life and peace, not guilting us to do more, be more, or behave better. If guilt shows up as a performance enhancer, it's a lie straight from the enemy, whose sole delight is to steal and destroy. This enemy would love nothing better than to keep women of faith tied up in guilty knots so they're unable to shine brightly for God. (See Romans 8:6.)

Like a piece of fake money, counterfeit guilt may look and smell like the real thing at first glance but will bring nothing but disappointment and grief if you try to use it to improve your life.

Post-Comma Drama

As we listen to those voices in our heads, we begin to craft a personal story. Before long, we've polished a set of post-comma words, the nice, little list you offer when someone asks, "Who are you and what do you do?" They're the short story of your identity, which is, after all, just the story you tell yourself and others about who you are.

So, what's your post-comma story?

> "I'm Beth, and I'm a mom, a hiker, a creative,
> and a civil servant."
> (*Wait, civil servants can be creative?*)

> "I'm Julianne, and I'm a successful, thin, happy,
> gorgeous model wife with two perfect children."
> (*No one likes Julianne much.*)

"I'm Trish, and I'm a Sunday school teacher,
welcome desk receptionist, member of the prayer
team, and women's ministry volunteer."
(*That's a lot of time spent at church!*)

"I'm Candace, and I'm a recent divorcée with
three kids and a home-based photography business
I'm determined to keep afloat."
(*Candace needs lots of hugs.*)

If you'd asked me for my post-comma words a few years ago, I'd have offered: wife. daughter. sister to six. creative. cook. church goer. perfectionist. organizer. leader. introvert. good girl. teacher. reader.

I grew up in a Christian home with parents who loved me and made sure I was in church before I was even potty-trained. Early on I discovered that life works best when you follow the rules.

As the oldest, I was responsible for lots of diaper-changing and babysitting. I made good grades and found my niche in the fine arts program. I enjoyed band and choir and entered competitions galore. In the college and grad school scene, I held down a job, practiced my music for twelve hours or more a week, led my sorority, and studied hard.

I basically always did what was expected of me (and then a little more, just to be sure). If there'd been an award for "quintessential good girl," I'd have had one hanging on my wall.

Life was predictable and manageable, and my identity story helped me keep it that way.

You're probably wondering about my identity story at this point. Can I share a secret first? I've always secretly loved the phrase, "You are what you eat." Corny, I know, but I giggle when I imagine how ridiculous we'd look if we ever turned into what we love to eat. Picture crunchy footsteps and a fabulous, triangular, orange outfit should I ever become my favorite potato chip. "You are what you eat" sounds similar to the main identity story I claimed for most of my life. With all of my responsibilities, good performance, and desire to be excellent, my main story became: **You are what you *do*.**

I was an exceptional doer. A committed perfectionist. An over-the-top achiever. The "do" mantra ruled my life, and quite happily too! You could've condensed my post-comma words to:

Janna, Proud Purveyor of the
Performance-Driven Life.

How'd that turn out for me? Yeah, not so great.

I pretty much worked really hard for a really long time until I got so tired and burned out that I couldn't do one . . . more . . . thing. It wasn't exactly the life of great significance and joy I'd hoped for.

But, we're skipping to the middle of the story. Let me back up and tell you how I got there.

What Upended My Neat, Little World

By the time I'd left college, I'd learned to live my "You are what you do" story like a rock star. I married the best man on the planet, convinced that if I tried hard enough ours would be the perfect marriage. Dave and I would do everything right, starting with dedicating the first years of our marriage to serving God in the ministry. A life tithe, of sorts. So, off we went to wet our feet in full-time ministry.

God created me with a deep passion for getting things done, and I've always lived life at a delightfully furious pace. I'm just happiest doing something. So, what was I doing in ministry? What *wasn't* I doing is the better question!

I enjoyed pimply faces staring back at me five days a week and even spent summer hours designing bulletin boards, scouting out interesting field trips, and creating unusual projects to engage teenaged minds. (Comic strip analysis for *Beowulf*, anyone?) I thrived designing invitations and making cookies for the scrapbooking nights I pioneered in the women's ministry. Pop in on me on a Saturday and you'd probably find me surfing Pinterest for a new recipe to try at the next young married couples' party we were hosting in our home. And on Sunday you could wave at me tickling the ivories during services or racing to choir practice after my afternoon nap.

I even gleefully brainstormed extra work for fun, like founding the drama department at our high school. Everything from script to casting to set design to costumes to ticket sales—

you name it, I tackled it with abandon. Sure, it was a lot of work. Sure, it was outside of my normal job description. But, the students adored it, and the audiences were thrilled to be entertained by people they knew. We were successes under those bright lights and shiny costumes.

My heart soared when I was busy. I loved serving in ministry and making a difference. And I was doing what mattered most: glorifying God, which I knew pleased Him. I was wife to one, sister to six, daughter to two, and minister to all. And I did all of it passionately because I live life that way.

Are you familiar with the phrase "rough patch"?

Before long the ministry hit one of those, only it was less of a patch than a brick wall to crash through with a cliff right behind it. Think worst-case scenario. The lead pastor, school administrator, and head executive assistant ("Been here twenty years and practically run the place") exited at the same time. What was left? A giant plot twist where anyone who was still around stared at each other with the what-do-we-do-now question on trembling lips and panic in their wide, bright eyes.

What would you do if all of your hard work were about to come crashing down and what you'd built was teetering on the brink of disaster? A good Performance-Driven-Life girl would double her efforts and plug the holes.

Of course, that's what I did. And my too-busy life turned into, "Survive this, sucker!"

It was a hunker-down, work-longer-hours, never-let-em-see-you-sweat situation. I hope you've never lived through anything like it, but if you have, you know you're clueless in the midst of it. When you're stuck in survival mode, you can't process the toll it takes on you. All I knew was God wanted me to serve, and I didn't want the people I was serving to suffer. I desperately desired to hold things together so the ministry would continue well. My Performance-Driven-Life (PDL) gene was in overdrive.

But the constant furious pace meant things started to slip. I'd forget an appointment, miss a deadline, or run out of time and energy for the next project. The Twin Terrors began to have a heyday with me.

As I sat in church one night, my eyelids lowered on their own and my head nodded forward. I sat up quickly and peered out of the corner of my eye to see if anyone had noticed. Then my eyelids slipped shut again, and I was back to the jerk-and-peek game. I wanted to huff out loud, but instead angrily asked God, "Is this what you really meant for your servants? Is this what you expect of us? I'm working so hard for you every single day that I can't even stay awake. I'm supposed to enjoy Your Word and worship You, but I can't because I'm too exhausted! Is this really what you intended the Christian life to be like?"

I didn't dare share these thoughts with anyone, of course. When you're knee-deep in survival mode you don't think to ask for help or don't have the bandwidth to find someone who actually will. Besides, even if I'd had someone to ask, I feared platitudes, pity, and judgment. I was afraid to be seen as anything less than a good servant of God. After all, the truly godly ones "take up their cross daily" (Luke 9:23) and are glad "to

Do You Hear What I Hear

spend and be spent" (2 Corinthians 12:15) for the gospel, right? Verses like these fueled my impressive doing. *Good* Christians can handle anything. Who was I to complain?

So, I kept on busying in my PDL.

Where the PDL Left Me

Growing up we never had pets. One of my brothers suffered severe allergies, the kind where your throat swells up if you eat a nut and your skin breaks into nasty sore patches if you live with anything furry or feathery.

Imagine my surprise and trepidation when my husband of five years started to hint about a puppy. I laughed the first couple times, then raised my eyebrows when he brought it up again. To my inexperienced eye, pets seemed like a lot of work. It didn't help that any time we mentioned a puppy to anyone we knew we heard horror stories of chewed shoes, wet rugs, and all-night howling. (Why do people insist on leading with the worst stories instead of the good ones?)

We adopted a nine-week-old Maltese-Yorkie who became a lesson in pets, laughter, and patience for me. Buster was the cutest, fluffiest little ball of mischief you'd ever meet and a smart little bugger too! One of his favorite puppy antics was to sneak into our bedroom, steal a pair of my pantyhose, and race gleefully for the guest room, pantyhose waving like a flag. There he'd crawl under the bed and shred my poor hose into stringy pieces.

Buster was a very high-energy dog who needed long walks. Living in Florida, the walks were warm affairs. Even in the early morning, you'd sweat two steps down the driveway. That never deterred our little rat though. He loved to race to the end of the leash, sniff everything in sight, and leave a "Buster was here" mark on every bush, tree, fire hydrant, and large rock within reach.

When you opened the door to let him back into the house, Buster would rush to his water dish and sloppily lap as fast as he could, then plop full length on the cool linoleum, tongue hanging from the side of his mouth. If you called his name, he'd move his eyes toward you but not so much as lift his head. He was just too hot and tuckered out to bother.

Within a few months of holding a floundering ministry together, I felt like Buster after a long walk in the Florida sunshine. It wasn't just the external pressure of all I was doing, though, that was enough to make a grown woman collapse. It was the internal pressure that was the worst, the voices inside my head that pushed me to the breaking point.

Of course, you and I both know the impossibility of perfect performance. But, boy did I try. No one experiencing pressure, stress, and over-the-top expectations like I was should expect anything less than shouting head voices, and believe me, mine could've won awards.

You messed up again.

You should be doing better.

Yeah, you're right to worry about that!

You better do more.

You need to be perfect.

What will people think?

You ought to live up to expectations.

I looked around at my life in all of its sticky, busy glory and wondered what to do with the plates that dropped and shattered, with the people who turned away in despair because I couldn't help enough, or with the whispers that the ministry was faltering no matter how hard I tried. From that vantage point I had not even an ounce of trouble believing the voice that boomed,

You're not good enough.

I swallowed the story whole, and it burned all the way down, choking me half to death.

Breaking Point

I lived this "not good enough" story for months, hounded by the Twin Terrors, and holding my secret shame inside. I didn't know how to tell anyone about it or even find someone who'd be able to handle my gory reality. Besides, I was proficient with masks. The "I'm fine" was a favorite, followed closely by "Got this under control" and "One more thing? No sweat!" I never left home without at least one mask, and they shielded me as I silently suffered.

I tried to push "You're not good enough" to the cobwebbed corners of my mind. Deep weariness blanketed me and discouragement settled in. I was physically, emotionally, and mentally tired. Tired of:

- feeling alone.
- receiving too little help.
- assuming I could indefinitely maintain current activity levels.
- shouldering a burden that was too big and heavy.
- bumping into others' egos and complaints.
- hiding my secret shame.
- fighting my insecurities.
- trying to live up to elusive expectations.

I grew fragile and brittle, stretched to the point where I might snap any second. Near the end of May we held a graduation planning meeting with the staff. Two teachers interrupted throughout the meeting, giving their opinions on every minute detail. If you've ever sat through a meeting like that, you know how excruciating and mind-numbing that process becomes. I'm not typically a tantrum thrower, but I got so angry I snapped at both of them and quit the meeting. If there'd been a door nearby I would've slammed it at least twice for good measure.

Blessedly, reprieve came with our summer break and a trip out of town to my brother's graduation. I'll never forget the night I returned home. I hadn't even retracted the handle to my rolling suitcase before my husband, Dave, stopped me with a serious face and the words, "We need to talk."

Think of all of the plot twists that begin with that short sentence: dissolved relationships, financial despair, broken dreams, split families. You can imagine, then, the stomach lurch and instant sweat that occurred with those words.

We sat knee-to-knee on the couch. Dave began, "This last year has been brutal on both of us. We've put in long hours, trying to hold things together in this ministry. It's been a ton of work and has taken a toll on us physically and spiritually. It's been tough on our marriage too.

I've been doing a lot of thinking while you were gone and realized that God never meant for life to taste like cardboard. I believe He's used this past year to show us He intends a better way. *We need to leave this ministry.*"

Even as I watched my entire world shift, I didn't burst into tears or argue or flip out. I sat in stunned silence, too confused by what I felt. I wasn't worried what would happen to the ministry if we left. I wasn't sad to leave friends and people whom we loved. I wasn't scared to pack an entire household. I wasn't even apprehensive about where we'd live. All of that would come later.

In that course-altering moment, all I felt was *intense relief* . . . and the tiniest spark of hope.

I guess you could say I was finally tired enough.

{2}

When You Get Tired Enough

A month after the epic "We need to talk" moment, Dave and I packed our bags and flew to Colorado for a survey trip. We had no idea where we would live, how we'd pay the bills, or what church we'd find. For three weeks we drove the I-25 corridor from Longmont to Colorado Springs, shaking hands with pastors, delivering resumes, and touring homes for rent.

We'd been trolling Craigslist for a couple of weeks when Dave stumbled upon a rental in the foothills about forty minutes southwest of Denver. It boasted incredible views, a mountaintop location, and a decent price. Dave was convinced we needed to see this house. I finally agreed, but only because I felt like a sweet, submissive wife that day. Silently I vowed, *No way are we living there! I am not moving to some scary high mountain in the middle of nowhere.*

The drive to the house reinforced my fears. Switchbacks and hairpins and drop-offs, oh my! I white-knuckled the armrest all the way up to eighty-three hundred feet above sea level with my heart in my throat.

Walking into the house, we were surprised by warm wood floors and a second-floor master with balcony. Oh, but the kitchen . . . I fell a little bit in love the moment my eyes took in the double ovens, wrap-around island, smooth granite, and more counter space than any sane woman knows what to do with.

The pièce de résistance, though, was an enormous, bi-level deck, complete with hot tub and 180° views of Denver and the surrounding foothills that took your breath away. You could see for sixty miles as the property sloped away, the mountain air tickled your nose, and the aspen leaves rustled.

We were standing on the second-floor deck, enjoying the view and the breeze, when a loud clacking under our feet startled us. "What was that?" we asked the agent.

Before he could answer, a large buck leisurely strolled from underneath the deck. The deer turned and looked at us for a few seconds before regally striding away.

"Oh." The agent laughed. "You'll see lots of wildlife around here."

On the drive down the mountain, Dave asked me, "So what do you think?" What came out of my mouth surprised us both and segued us into the next scene of the story God was writing with our lives.

A Change in Focus

Do you remember Mary and Martha in the Bible? These two sisters host Jesus and his disciples in their home. The story unfolds with Mary sitting among the boys in the living room soaking up Jesus's words while Martha scurries around the kitchen like a whirlwind, checking the roast lamb, setting the table, and finishing the cake.

I've always had a soft spot for Martha. Here's this poor woman trying to serve dinner for fifteen or more with zero help. She flies past the living room and sees her sister, Mary, at Jesus's feet, and that's the last straw. I can just hear Martha's frustrated thoughts: *How dare she do this to me? My own sister! Doesn't she see that I'm doing everything on my own?!*

Martha's a smart cookie, though. She marches right up to the highest authority in the room and tells Jesus, "Make my sister come and help me."

Don't you just feel for Martha? I wish I could reach into that story and magically drop three capable women in the kitchen: one to set the table, one to chop veggies, and one to take the drink orders (because that would've been a job on its own). I'd tell Martha to go sit beside her sister because dinner is under control.

Maybe I empathize with Martha because, like her, I'm a doer. Maybe I need it to be okay that I like to serve too. I've sometimes secretly wondered, *If we women sit at Jesus's feet all day, how long until our world runs out of clean clothes and dies of starvation?*

Have you ever had rebel thoughts like those?

I know, I know. When Jesus told Martha she was distracted with much serving, He wasn't advocating literally sitting at His feet so you neglect your family or refuse to help a suffering friend. There's a deeper message.

When we look beneath the surface, we realize Martha's serving was frantic because she fell victim to misdirected focus. Jesus tells her, "Martha, Martha, you are anxious and troubled about many things" (Luke 10:41). Martha's perception was off, and it created stress in her life. She was stressed because she was caught up in her doing. Her post-comma words probably condensed to "Chief Cook and Hostess," and so she spent her time serving but mildly confused about the sit-with-God-or-serve-dinner-now issue. And that story led her to pressure The Way, The Truth, and The Life for some sister help ASAP.

The rubber meets the road for us here too. Let's face it: if something needs to be done, we women are often the ones to do it. We've been trained to expect life this way. We're used to doing it all: keeping the family content, the house clean, the boss happy, the friend comforted, the mom up-to-date, the meals cooked, the dog walked, the science projects made . . . [pant, pant, pant]. The voices confirm what we suspect: "This is just life. And, if it doesn't work the first time, just throw a little more effort at it." Sound familiar?

But when we have a misdirected focus, we remain stuck in the stories we've always lived. We strive to live up to the post-comma words of Perfect Wife, Model Daughter, Brilliant Career

Woman, Unstoppable Mom, Sole Provider, Uncomplaining Caregiver that have been handed to us by culture, family, and religion because those are the stories we know best. They fit like a well-worn shoe.

Besides, who has the time to stop and examine a post-comma story with so much *life* happening around her?

But, might we take a second here to ponder our stories? It won't take long, I promise. Just answer one quick question. How do you finish this equation?

_____ = good Christian and significant life

Being a good mom? Leading Bible study? Mentoring women? Serving at church? Volunteering with the homeless? Focusing on family above everything? Becoming a prayer warrior? Practicing the spiritual disciplines? Loving God first?

What equals true godliness to you? How you fill that blank reveals the truth of your main post-comma story.

Not What We Expected

There's a story tucked into John's gospel where Jesus escapes from the crowd after miraculously feeding the five thousand with a couple loaves of bread and a few fish. He's "hiding" to have some rest and alone time with his Dad. Eventually, the crowd finds Jesus, and I picture Him smiling because He knows all about their fabulous Sherlock skills. "How'd you get here without a boat?" they ask. (Hint: It involved some middle-of-the-night water-walking.) Jesus knows they're mainly interested in His culinary genius, so He answers them with a food metaphor.

> Truly, truly, I say to you, you are seeking me, not because you saw signs, but because you ate your fill of the loaves. Do not work for the food that perishes, but for the food that endures to eternal life, which the Son of Man will give to you. (John 6:26–27)

The crowd pauses then asks Him a telling question: "What must we do, to be doing the works of God?" (John 6:28).

Our ears perk with curiosity and our overworked hearts leap, excited to hear what Jesus will say next. "Here it comes," we think. "I just know it. Now we'll hear the truth behind the mystery of what God expects and what we should *do* for Him!"

Jesus answers them—and us, "This is the work of God, that you believe in him whom he has sent" (John 6:29).

Stink! I was hoping for something a bit more list-like, weren't you? A few "thou shalts" and maybe a "shalt not" or two?

But Jesus came to debunk all that. He came to fulfill the law, not add to it. He took care of the heavy lifting so we could stop trying, and He wants to exchange our effort and striving for something better.

> Come unto me, all you who labor and are heavy laden and I will give you rest. Take my yoke upon you and learn of me

for I am meek and lowly in heart and you will find rest for your souls. For my yoke is easy, and my burden is light. (Matthew 11:28–30)

Jesus understood what we often miss in the midst of our busy: *no one "does" just because.* The deep-down motive behind try-hard doing is a search for something. We may tell ourselves, "I do for others because I want to help," or, "I just have a heart for people," or, "I serve to glorify God and show that I love Him." But if we look deeply enough into our hearts, we will find that any standard of doing we hold onto stems from a longing for worth and significance.

The answer is never in the doing. Excessive doing only leaves us like Martha: weary, depleted, wishing for help, and a smidge angry. No one can sustain long-term performance without getting tuckered out. The only cure for a try-hard PDL is to come to Jesus and rest. And the only time you actually stop for rest is when you're finally tired enough.

Come Away and Rest

When Dave and I returned to the car after drooling over a 180° view, a vast kitchen, and the cozy atmosphere of the mountain house rental, he opened the conversation with a hopeful voice. "So what do you think?"

I started to say, "The house is beautiful, but it's too far away from everything, not to mention at the top of a mountain! It's crazy to think we could ever live there."

But in the instant before the words formed in my mouth, Psalm 23:2 popped into my head: "He makes me lie down in green pastures. He leads me beside still waters. He restores my soul." What actually came out of my mouth was, "Did you feel how peaceful and quiet it was? I think God wants to give us rest in that house." I still can't fully explain how I had one thought while God spoke another through me and convinced me it was true. It was the weirdest experience.

I think my soul just felt God wooing me from my Martha-ness and inviting me to rest. He knew that retreating and resting were what I desperately needed, and, of course, He was right. Thankfully, He'd already prepared the perfect, peaceful place for rest to begin.

The Unrest of Rest

Within a week we'd rented the mountain house. Within a month we'd packed an entire life, driven over seventeen hundred miles, gone from sea level to over eighty-three hundred feet in altitude, and officially begun a season of rest.

Dave found a job right away, but I didn't. It was fine with me because I needed a break. In the crazy of all I'd been doing, there hadn't been much energy left for Bible reading and prayer time. Guilt harped on me there, and truthfully, I missed communing with God.

So with this new season of rest, God and I renewed our

relationship. Many mornings I'd sit for an hour or more in our comfy leather recliner with my Bible and notebook, drinking in the awe-inspiring view, feasting on the Word, and chatting with the Lord.

We started with Psalm 23, and as I pondered "restores my soul," God did the work behind the words. Slowly my sore, overworked heart began to heal.

I stayed hidden away in our mountain house for a while because I couldn't face the thought of community or serving. It was all too fresh and raw. As the months passed, though, the desire to be connected and serve again grew.

I auditioned for a local community theater putting on a production of *The Christmas Carol*, thinking it would be a fun, low-key way to ease back into community. However, my audition was such a colossal, magnificent, show-stopping success that the sympathetic director invented a non-speaking role for me so I could participate without botching the entire show. Needless to say, I declined the pity part.

Retreating to the mountain house to lick my wounds, it took a few weeks before I found the courage to venture out again, this time to a more familiar scene: church. I joined the handbell choir on a whim because it sounded pretty fun and stress-free. It felt good to be part of a community, serving with music again.

As the church women and I became better acquainted, their enthusiastic ideas began to flow.

"You play the piano, Janna? Oh, pretty please, will you fill in for me next Sunday?"

"You sing? You should join the choir!"

"You used to teach? We desperately need help in the children's program."

"You work from home? I need someone with loads of free time to help me throw the annual Women's Tea."

I didn't immediately jump at all of the opportunities, and it didn't take more than a guilt trip or two in my direction to cause a strong reaction on my part—a godly, sophisticated reaction, of course.

I was spitfire mad.

I thought, *Here I am barely reentering life and ministry, and you people are pushing me to do all of these things. No way am I gonna let you drag me back into the same kind of crazy overwork I just escaped!* So I ran back to my peaceful mountain house as fast as I could.

Why Nothing Worked

Around that time I'd begun reading the Gospels. I love the stories of Jesus's miracles and teaching and had become intrigued by the Pharisees. As I ran home from church, Guilt hard on my heels, I told God, "I think these people who keep telling me what I should do for You are Pharisees!" The thought stemmed from part self-righteous anger and part God's perfect timing.

I began an in-depth study of the Pharisees. The more I learned about these righteous pillars of "doing for God," the more my indignation grew, and the more convinced I became that the people I'd met at church looked eerily similar to these Bible characters.

Then came the Crisis Point, the moment of truth when God swept away every single one of my post-comma labels.

One day after I'd been studying for a while, validated in my anger and self-righteous in my conclusions, God gently turned my face toward the very Pharisees that disturbed me: the people who tried so hard to please Him perfectly, the only ones whose lifestyle and beliefs Jesus fiercely chastised. God pointed my face toward them and said:

> *Yes, you are right. These Christians I've put in front of you want you to prove your acceptability and righteousness by what you do, just like Pharisees. That's how they view life and how they view Me. And that's the same thing you've done your whole life. You've lived judging yourself and others by what you do. You view the Christian life through a Pharisee lens.*

As I write these words, my head sinks and my eyes fill. I remember the sheer horror and shame that engulfed me when God showed me I was just like the holier-than-thous Jesus scathingly rebuked. I had been basing all of my goodness and worth on what I did, striving for God's acceptance, living the Performance-Driven Life as if my life depended on it.

My entire world crumbled in that moment. I looked around in shock as my beliefs about Christianity came crashing down. Everything I knew to be true about how to think, live, react, serve, be godly and acceptable—basically, how to function in the Christian life—was knocked out from under me, demolished into a heap of rubble at my feet.

Devastation overtook me as the thought dawned: *Everything you've based your life on has been a lie. You have no clue how to live Christianity for real.*

I had nothing left. No way to define myself. Nothing I knew for certain. Nothing I was sure would work.

What would you do if your entire world crumbled and your most deeply held beliefs came crashing down around you? How would you react if your entire life turned out to be false?

You'd probably plop down on the floor and cry. For a week straight. Then you'd plunge into depression because you have nothing to hold on to, nothing you feel you can trust, and no hope of fixing it.

And that's exactly what I did.

But God . . .

When God said it was time for a new story, I'd accepted the challenge and did what had always worked for me: I threw a little more effort at the problem. I tried every way I could to write a new story. I rested. I immersed myself in the Word. I renewed my relationship with Him. I dove into church with hands stretched to serve.

It wasn't until God showed me my Pharisee glasses that I realized I'd been chasing the impossible. Oh, I desperately wanted a new story; I craved it like chocolate cake during a hormonal week. But in that moment of truth, I saw clearly for the first time that I would never be able to rewrite my story on my own. It wasn't for lack of willingness or lack of trying. I simply had no idea where to begin, much less what the story might be.

So in that gut-wrenching, heartbreaking moment when I came face-to-face with the truth that I was like the people Jesus staunchly opposed, I clung to the very last thing I had left. With tears streaming down my cheeks, head bowed, and hands folded like a little girl, I prayed like I never had before.

> *God, I don't know which end is up right now.*
> *You've knocked away everything I thought I knew.*
> *How am I supposed to live the Christian life?*
> *What do I even believe anymore?*
> *You promised, "If any of you lack wisdom, let him ask of God."*
> *Well, I'm seriously lacking right now, and I have nowhere to turn.*
> *I don't know what else to do, so if you don't help,*
> *I may as well give up because I'll never figure it out on my own.*
> *Show me the truth, God.*
> *Show me what to believe.*
> *Give me the wisdom I desperately seek.*
> *You're all I have left.*

I prayed for days, knee-deep in a fear, confusion, and desolation I'd never experienced.

And because He's a God who never lies . . .
Because He's the lover of our souls . . .
Because He understood even better than I did how
   desperately tired I truly was . . .
And because, best of all, He knew I was finally ready
   for the answer . . .
He prepared a most unlikely source to lavish the truth
   on me.

In the middle of a dreary, underwhelming Friday morning, surrounded by filmy shower doors and mildewed grout, the best news in the world fell on my tuckered-out, thirsty heart for the very first time.

{3}

The Lavish Heart of Grace

Wouldn't it be great if God made life-altering moments glamorous? Maybe an angelic chorus, or handwriting on the wall, or even a massive power surge so the lights flicker, or something? At the very least it would help us know to sit up and pay attention. But that's not His style. He's more into the ordinary moments when the atmosphere is quiet enough to hear His still small voice.

The day that changed everything for me started as an ordinary, bleary Friday morning. No bells rang. No whistles blew. No angels appeared in shiny white to give me great news while I tried not to wet my pants. Instead, with a spray bottle in one hand, a Mr. Clean® Magic Eraser in the other, filmy shower doors in front of me, and the quiet buzz of the speaker plugged into my iPad, I listened to a man talk about "When You Get

Tired Enough."

I knew I was tired enough—tired of the drama, tired of the over-busy, tired of constant doing, tired of being hurt, tired of trying things that didn't work, and sick and tired and ashamed of my Pharisee life.

God has such a sense of humor, and I believe He wanted to make sure I'd never forget this life-altering moment. The talk was recorded by a man I'd never heard of. It was recommended to me by one of my brothers with whom I rarely discussed spiritual truth. I was neither the intended nor the live audience. And I encountered it during one of my least favorite tasks in the world: bathroom-cleaning. Added together, these random events had God's fingerprints all over them. He knew this was precisely what my tuckered-out, little PDL heart needed, and He had planned this seemingly ordinary moment on purpose.

Have you ever been concerned that a teacher somehow knew your inner thoughts and was singling you out of the crowd? That's how I felt that day. For the first time in my life, I heard:

Someone will try to tell you that with enough effort you can (and should) be able to do more and be more as a sold-out, fired-up, walkin'-worthy, whole-hearted servant of Jesus Christ. And that person will tell you techniques to perform in order to be that kind of Christian.

And you'll try so hard, but it won't work. You'll fail. And you'll get cynical and jaded and mad. So, you'll start "playing religion" and put on a mask and walk around pretending. But inside you'll be burned out and frustrated and disillusioned. And eventually you'll begin to believe that God doesn't work.

I winced in agreement. The stories made me wonder if the man was using scenes from my life for his illustrations. My heart gasped for air until I heard:

But what if it isn't necessary to do so much for God? What if the best way to live life is actually the same way you accepted eternal life—by grace? *Are you going to be sanctified and "grow up" by the flesh or by grace and identity in Christ?*[1]

All of my life I'd viewed Christianity through the tint of "You are only as good as what you do." My "religion" had been a try-hard, do-more effort based on what I thought God expected of believers. My Pharisee glasses colored Scripture with a "do" filter, causing me to view Christianity as a command to be followed, a project to be completed, and a list to be checked off. So, the better I conquered each "task," the better I felt about myself and my godliness.

When I looked at life through Pharisee glasses, I measured my success and significance *by what I did*, I judged myself and others *based on performance*, and I viewed God through the same tint, as if He thought, "I'll be happy with her as long as she behaves and serves well."

My entire life I'd been convinced that I could prove my

worth—to God, to me, and to everybody else—*by what I do.*

Yikes! When I condense my belief system into a few paragraphs, it sounds so misguided and petty. As if anyone could ever be good enough, do enough, or serve enough to prove anything to God.

But the day my worn-out, overworked heart heard, "Are you going to be sanctified and 'grow up' by the flesh or by grace and identity in Christ?" God peeled away my Pharisee glasses for good and showed me the truth. As I listened to words by a man I didn't know, from a place I'd never been, through a source I'd never imagined, during a chore I'd never liked, God whispered,

This is it, kid.
This is the truth you've begged Me for:
grace for LIFE.

My whole body sighed in relief as my heart cried, *Yes,* and the Holy Spirit affirmed, *Grace is the truth you seek.* The instant I chose to believe, my feet froze, my Magic Eraser stilled, and goose bumps raced up my arms. Life would never be the same again because grace changes everything.

Grace Discovered

Most of us are familiar with the word "grace." We know "for by grace are ye saved through faith" (Romans 6:23 KJV). But, after conversion, grace becomes the vague "something I need daily" or the nebulous "thing that gives me strength."

Often in real life, we see examples of grace misunderstood. My business friend, Amelia, and I scheduled a coffee meeting for a Thursday morning. I arrived early and saw Amelia and her assistant peering at a laptop together, so I ordered my coffee and found a place to fiddle with my phone while trying not to worry about all the work still piled on my desk. I wanted to meet with Amelia, but my foot jiggled impatiently the longer I sat there alone.

About fifteen minutes after our meeting was scheduled to begin, Amelia hurried over with a profuse apology. Before we'd exchanged more than two sentences though, her phone rang. She whipped it out of her pocket, glanced at the screen and said, "I *really* need to take this. Thanks so much for your grace!" My mouth dropped open as she turned away, phone already at her ear.

Grace is often misunderstood as the nice things Christians do for each other, something we just expect from believers and often take unfair advantage of.

But the grace that God gives is so much more than the watery version we've encountered before. Like a mystery package under the Christmas tree with your name lovingly written on the tag, grace is a beautiful, free gift that's infinitely more than a pretty bow, cheery paper, and a curiously shaped box.

Grace is an awe-inspiring gift, and to begin to appreciate it, much less fully grasp it, we must shake it, peer at it, smell it, turn it over, and tap it on the table. Even after the unwrapping, grace may still defy words because we've never held anything quite like it before.

In fact, we cannot begin to fully comprehend or embrace grace until we have taken a good, long look at The Giver. Understanding grace means sweeping away stodgy religious connotations and leftover Christianese clinging to the word. Diving into grace means going deeper into its very heart where we discover Someone Else's heart.

For at the very center of grace is the heart of a Father. A Father who created you, who wants you, who longs for deep relationship with you. A Father who knew exactly how unimpressive, mundane, try-hard, or scandalous your life would be. A Father who looks at all the muck and says, "She's infinitely precious to me and so very worth rescuing!" A Father who pours out His heart, lavishing grace on you in the highest form of love you and I will ever know: the sacrifice of His perfect Son.

For there, at the very heart of grace, we find the lavish, ineffable love of God.

Love Defined

Have you ever heard the word "ineffable"? I stumbled over it a few months ago, and since I have an ongoing love affair with words, I looked it up. According to Webster, ineffable means, "Too great or extreme to be expressed in words."[2] I instantly knew this word belonged in front of "love of God." The deeper you dive into God's love, the more you realize you hardly grasp it at all! Mere words scarcely do justice to a love so deep and long and wide and high that even if we spend the rest of our lives getting lost in it, we'll still have barely skimmed a bucketful off the surface of a great and mighty river.

But that doesn't mean we don't try. That doesn't mean we won't drink deeply. It just means that after we've drunk from Living Water, we'll write a new favorite word, "ineffable," on the front of our insignificant bucket in the hopes that others will stop and taste for themselves too.

Here are a few ways to describe what I have tasted and seen of enormous, too-great-and-extreme-to-be-expressed-in-mere-words Love—my bucket that I offer for you to take your own sip.

Grand

God's love is grander than any human love we've ever seen, experienced, or offered. His love is so wide that you can never reach the other side of it. It's so deep that once you jump in, you'll drown forever in its depths. His love is so high that no pole vault or plane or catapult or rocket can reach beyond it. It's so long that you'll never outgrow or outlast it. (Ephesians 3:18)

Free

God's love is one hundred percent, no strings attached, no-need-to-work-for-it, free of charge. He loves you because He *wants* to love you, not because of anything you can do to deserve it or earn it. He loves you freely because His love is too precious and vast for any of us to ever hope to pay for it anyway. And He extends this love to you passionately and unconditionally. If God were into commercial guarantees, His would be the first and last to truthfully claim: "God's love: always free, one hundred percent guaranteed!" (Ephesians 2:4–5, 8–9; John 15:9)

Steadfast

God's love never changes. He is completely and totally head over heels for you no matter the day, no matter the hour, no matter what you happen to mess up or overcome at any particular moment. His love is the same. Always and forever. Period. (Psalm 136, Lamentations 3:22)

Active

God's love is in motion. Because God loves, He gives—freely, abundantly, above anything we ever ask or think. God so loves that He gave His Son for you, to redeem you, to forgive you, to restore you. And this Active Lover calls you, woos you, pursues you, and desires you to receive and bask in His great love. (John 3:16, Romans 5:8, John 1:12)

Pro You

God's love is for *you*. His love is not indiscriminate, blindly covering all in its path. God's love is purposeful and highly selective. And He picked *you*! He longs for you and desires you. What's behind all of that love is a desire for relationship, for the two of you to communicate, to enjoy each other, and to be together forever.

God's love is also *for* you. He loves you so much that He is always on your side, rooting for you, wanting you to savor His best life for you. His love desires a full and victorious life for you right now. God's love is PRO YOU. (1 John 4:9, Romans 8:31–39)

Who He Is

What's more, this grand, unstoppable love stems from a place that makes jaws drop. God doesn't just love really, really well, like some kind of *amore* expert. Love is His identity, His character, His very essence. His love can never stall or morph or lessen or grow cold because love is His very identity. To use His own words, God is love! (1 John 4:16)

Love Displayed

Even though God tore away my Pharisee glasses in an instant, my grace journey was merely beginning, a journey that would redefine an old-school, stifling head knowledge of a concept I thought I understood but didn't.

What anchored the journey for me was realizing how much God loves me—no, not just realizing it—*experiencing* how much He loves me. Feeling it. Soaking in it. Plopping down in the middle of it and staying there.

I accepted Christ when I was in kindergarten. For most of my life, I could quote the verses and Bible stories about how much God loves us. But now I discovered the only way to own

God's love for me was to receive it deeply without reservation. To receive something you must experience it fully, not just with your head, but way down deep in your heart, where your emotions thrive and your True Self talks.

Try saying this phrase out loud: GOD LOVES ME.

How does that feel: difficult to trust? impossibly true? like it's meant for someone else? as if you've heard it before so what's the big deal?

I feel ya'. How can we expect anything other than skepticism or a watered-down version of "God loves me" when we never experience love like this anywhere else in our world? We have nothing familiar to compare to this type of love. Besides, our concept of a Heavenly Father's love is usually based on:

1. our own earthly fathers, and

2. what we've been taught by religion.

Let's be honest. For many of us, neither of the two has been a stellar example of love and grace.

1. Dads as Role Models for God. Once, I searched the house hollering "Mom!" as only a tween can do, loud enough to scare the neighbors. She wasn't answering. I cruised the kitchen, skidded into the laundry room, and peered out the window into the backyard. Where was she? When I finally made it to her bedroom at the back of the house, I heard scratching noises. Rounding the corner, I found my mom scrubbing the bathroom linoleum on her hands and knees with tears streaming down her face.

My heart constricted and I blurted, "Mom, what's wrong?

Why are you crying?"

She answered, "Oh, I'm just talking to the Lord, sweetie."

I cocked my head, glad that my mom loved Jesus so much but confused by how talking to Him made her cry so hard.

A couple of decades later I discovered that my mom had been praying passionately for her family: for her seven children, for herself, and especially for her husband, a man in the throes of addiction and entrenched in an emotional affair with a woman from church.

As a talented vocalist, gifted trombonist, and amazing conductor, my dad is a musical genius. He's the type of guy that can pick up any instrument and play it convincingly. A man who writes entire songs in his head. A man with a natural talent for music theory that the rest of the world devotes years to learning.

When I was six he finished his master's degree in conducting by directing a full orchestra and choir in Handel's "Hallelujah Chorus" completely from memory. A lot of Saturday mornings I'd wake up to repetitive piano-plunking. I'd shuffle into the den in my socks, and, yup, it was Dad, writing a new song, arranging full orchestration for a church choir piece, or crafting a medley for his brass ensemble off the top of his head.

Emotion plays a key role in effective music, and like many musicians my dad was sensitive. While I never doubted my dad's love for me, he was unpredictable. I quickly learned that doing everything right and being good kept him from being disappointed or upset with me.

Of course, it's foolish to measure any parent against a

standard of perfection. I don't mean to hold up an impossible standard here. I'm merely sharing some of my story for you to see where my concept of a Heavenly Father began.

2. *Religion Adds to the God Picture.* Religion offers another view of God. As is true in many churches, the messages we hear most often from the pulpit include some God-truth and some institutional preferences. The danger is that the two get all mashed together and come out looking like a single entity.

For me, the mash-up was a list of ways to be a godly Christian: a bunch of dos and don'ts.

- ✓ **Do** believe on the Lord Jesus Christ and be saved.
- ✓ **Don't** disrespect your parents.
- ✓ **Do** come to church whenever the doors are open.
- ✓ **Don't** wear slutty clothes.
- ✓ **Do** serve God in the church and community as often as possible.
- ✓ **Don't** have sex before marriage.
- ✓ **Do** be a good testimony for God.

All of the "doing" talk reinforced my growing belief that God is happier with you when you do what He wants, and what He wants most is for you to live a holy life. And how do you live a holy life? You keep your behavior in line by doing all of the things God expects of you and avoiding anything He warns against.

I melded what I knew of my own father and what I heard from religion into a picture of a God who loved me with strings attached. The God I saw was a supreme, all-knowing Being, sitting on a grand throne with a stern gaze, never smiling or laughing much—at least not in my direction. Some days I knew God sighed at my failures. Other times I was sure He shook His head in exasperation. Every now and then I glimpsed a Smiling Father, but the picture was quickly overshadowed by fear of disappointing Him.

My warped view stemmed from religious teaching and my own father who was never intended to be held up as an image of God. My view was also aided by the Father of Lies who loves nothing better than whispering that God is not as good as we thought. Just ask Eve. It was Satan's first and best lie, and it worked so well he's never stopped using it.

I held on to the mental image of a stern Supreme Ruler who, though He loved me enough to send His Son, was definitely having second thoughts now because "she can't get her act together." I sometimes wondered if He was sorry He saved me because He'd found out I wasn't really worth the trouble after all.

Until grace.

God pierced my soul with a love arrow more potent than anything Cupid could concoct, and my heart burst wide open from the sheer beauty and warmth of that love.

GOD loves me.

God **LOVES** me.

God loves **ME**.

I soaked in the "God loves me" concept for a while, letting it play with the corners of my heart. I tasted the words on my tongue and imagined, "What if they are really true?"

God began to unfold the truth that He loves us. Period. Even when you're a jerk to your best friend. Even when your tongue is acid. Even when you hate your boss. Even when you yell at your husband. Even when you polish off the Doritos and the cake. Even when you don't want to be around Him. Even when you wonder if you can still trust Him. God loves you scandalously no matter what!

As I was learning to experience this Astounding Love, I came across a verse:

> For you did not receive the spirit of slavery to fall back into fear, but you have received the Spirit of adoption as sons, by whom we cry, "Abba! Father!" (Romans 8:15).

My heart grew all shiny-eyed and hopeful as I considered the possibility, "If this is true, then God doesn't look like I always feared!"

I knew that I wanted to call God something else. I wanted a new name for Him that was less "stern cop" and more "Abba" (which translates as "daddy"). I could've thrown a party when I thought of "Poppa." I began to call God "Poppa" whenever we chatted and still call Him that today. It's my special name for Him, and I know it makes Him smile. Each time I use it, I remember that He's my furiously loving Father, and I'm His precious, adored daughter. Our relationship has changed forever.

God Doesn't Just Love You

Along the way grace began to reveal that when God loves, He doesn't love clinically like a dictionary definition. God *likes* us too! What if you have a Heavenly Father who not only loves you enough to save you from a horrible eternity apart from Him, but Who actually enjoys you, delights in you, and wants to be around you? What if you have a Father who truly *likes* you?

While it may seem a nuance at first glance, a definite distinction exists between love and like. My friend tells the story of a couple he knew in college. Kelsey shared a drama class with several other students. As often happens in those classes where you make a fool of yourself regularly, the group grew close and soon began hanging out after class time. Bob, Kelsey's fiancé, often joined the group.

One night the friends were leisurely chatting when Bob suddenly declared, "You know, Kelsey, I really like you."

"Oh, gimme a break, Bob. Come on, we know you love her," another guy groaned. "You're gonna marry her!"

"No, no, of course I love her," Bob agreed, "but I'm saying I really, really *like* her too . . . ."

You could've heard a pin drop in the beautiful pause that filled the room. Then one by one enlightened smiles slowly lit each face.

Why is it that our brains say, "Yeah, yeah, of course you love me," but "You like me" is harder to accept? For me, "like" conjures memories of lined notebook paper scribbled with "Check yes or no" tossed at your desk during study hall. That picture's not as far from reality as you might think. When you like a person, you want them around, you delight in them, you enjoy relationship with them, and you usually get a little goofy about it.

The same is true of God with you. He delights in you. He craves intimate relationship with you. He wants to be around you. Did you know God adores His children so much He writes songs about them? Zephaniah 3:17 reveals that God delights over His own with singing. See if that doesn't conjure some fun mental pictures of guitars, second-floor windows, and late-night crooning from all the sappy movies you've ever seen. God is so glad that you are you, He sings about it to any angel who will listen! God loves you madly, and He plain ol' likes you too.

Love Received

God adores you this very minute, exactly as you are. Whether you've experienced His love yet or not. Whether you trust Him or not. Whether you're a good Christian, a blatant heathen, or somewhere in between. He loves you with an ineffable, enormous, unchanging love.

He longs for you to experience His love, to soak it deeply into your heart, and to receive it as yours. And do you know what happens when God's love trickles down from a practical head knowledge into your heart? Brennan Manning observed this transformation firsthand.

Back in the late 1960s, I was teaching at a university in Ohio and there was a student on campus who by society's standards would've been called ugly. He was short, extremely obese, he had a terrible case of acne, a bad lisp, and his hair was growing like Lancelot's horse – in four directions at one time. He wore the uniform of the day: a T-shirt that hadn't been washed since the Spanish American War, jeans with a butterfly on the back, and of course, no shoes.

In all my days, I have never met anybody with such low self-esteem. He told me that when he looked in the mirror each morning, he spit at it. Of course no campus girl would date him. No fraternity wanted him as a pledge. . . .

Christmas came along for Larry Malaney and he found himself back with his parents in Providence, Rhode Island. Larry's father is a typical lace-curtain Irishman. . . . A lace curtain Irishman, even on the hottest day in summer, will not come to the dining room table without wearing a suit, usually a dark pinstripe, starched white shirt, and a tie swollen at the top. He will never allow his sideburns to grow to the top of his ears and he always speaks in a low subdued voice.

Well, Larry comes to the dinner table that first night home, smelling like a billy goat. He and his father have the usual number of quarrels and reconciliations. And thus begins a typical vacation in the Malaney household. Several nights later, Larry tells his father that he's got to get back to school the next day.

"What time, son?"

"Six o'clock."

"Well, I'll ride the bus with you."

The next morning, the father and son ride the bus in silence. They get off the bus, as Larry has to catch a second one to get to the airport. Directly across the street are six men standing under an awning, all men who work in the same textile factory as Larry's father. They begin making loud and degrading remarks like, "Oink, oink, look at that fat pig. I tell you, if that pig was my kid, I'd hide him in the basement, I'd be so embarrassed." Another said, "I wouldn't. If that slob was my kid, he'd be out the door so fast, he wouldn't know if he's on foot or horseback. Hey, pig! Give us your best oink!"

In that moment, for the first time in his life, his father reached out and embraced him, kissed him on the lips, and said, "Larry, if your mother and I live to be two hundred years old, that wouldn't be long enough to thank God for the gift He gave to us in you. I am so proud that you're my son!"[3]

The transformation Larry underwent was nothing short of miraculous. You would've hardly believed this was the same guy. Larry cleaned himself up. He became fraternity president. He even began dating. Larry graduated with the highest GPA in the school's history, and soon afterwards was ordained and left for the foreign mission field to spread the love of Jesus with his life.

So, what changed Larry? What made the difference in the life of a boy who felt so insecure and unlovable? It wasn't getting an education that changed Larry. It wasn't doing more for God or going to in-depth counseling or even digging deeper into Scripture.

Larry's life was transformed when "his father looked deeply into his son's eyes, saw the good in Larry Malaney that Larry couldn't see for himself, affirmed him with a furious love, and changed the whole direction of his son's life."[4]

The furious love of God has a similar extraordinary effect on us. From a Father's heart filled to bursting for undeserving, hopeless performers like you and me comes a love so beautiful and full, it will knock you off your feet, bring tears to your eyes, and delight your soul as you absorb it deeply into your heart.

This lavish, ineffable love is the very heart of grace.

{4}

The Beautiful Truth of Grace

If you've spent much time in Christianity, you've been introduced to the concept of grace. But have you ever considered that grace is the foundational truth that sets Christianity apart from other religions?

During a British conference on comparative religions, experts from around the world debated what, if any, belief was unique to the Christian faith. They began eliminating possibilities. Incarnation? Other religions had different versions of gods appearing in human form. Resurrection? Again, other religions had accounts of return from death. The debate went on for some time until C. S. Lewis wandered into the room. "What's the rumpus about?" he asked, and heard in reply that his colleagues were discussing Christianity's unique contribution among world religions. Lewis responded, "Oh, that's easy. It's grace."

After some discussion, the conferees had to agree. The notion of God's love coming to us free of charge, no strings attached, seems to go against every instinct of humanity. The Buddhist eight-fold path, the Hindu doctrine of karma, the Jewish covenant, and the Muslim code of law – each of these offers a way to earn approval. Only Christianity dares to make God's love unconditional.[5]

When our minds try to grasp the enormity of grace, we have a hard time. Our brains stutter and shoot sparks: not the happy Fourth of July kind either, but the "Danger, overload imminent!" kind. Thankfully, Jesus spoke in parables so our poor heads would have a way to comprehend gigantic concepts like love and grace.

One of the most beautiful pictures of God's love and grace is found in the parable of the prodigal son. Luke records Jesus telling the story of a silly, selfish boy who demanded his inheritance, "Today, if you please," for a chance to see the world and try the things he secretly believed were more fulfilling than life with dad. The long-suffering father, a picture of great love, divides up his money and grants his son's request. Off the young man goes to explore and enjoy.

The Prodigal takes his journey as far from home as possible. Nothing is too expensive, outrageous, or beyond his reach. He is determined to have the full, fun life experience! It doesn't take long, though, to spend the inheritance, and any friends he's made disappear along with the money.

As often happens, circumstances take a turn for the worse. A natural disaster hits the country where he's living and creates widespread famine. With no money left, there's little the poor guy can do to combat soaring food prices. He is forced to beg for a job. At wit's end, he finally snags a demeaning, filthy job feeding pigs. The boy is so destitute that he gazes wistfully at the slop he feeds those smelly animals while his own stomach growls. But, no one gives him anything.

While he's mired in the muck of the pig pen, a thought occurs to him: *My father's servants get fed better than this.* He turns this over in his mind and decides that facing his father's wrath is worth it for a decent meal and a place to sleep that doesn't leave him smelling like a filthy barn.

When the bedraggled, friendless, penniless, sow-smelling ragamuffin trudges back to his father's house, what does Astounding Love do but dash out to meet him!

To say the son was shocked would be a bit of an understatement. See, on his way home, the Prodigal practiced what he would say to his dad. He'd had quite a long walk to mull it over, and I'm sure he winced as he contemplated all the ways he'd singlehandedly set the family business back a couple of decades. Talk about undeserving and inadequate.

He rehearses a heartfelt apology until he can get through it without choking up. He knows he doesn't deserve to be welcomed home and would never dare to ask for his old bedroom back. Gone is the arrogant, self-assured boy who demanded his inheritance. That boy has seen more of life than he ever cared to and knows what it is to suffer.

In spite of his own shock and bewilderment at seeing his father rush to meet him, the son remembers what he's practiced for miles and miles, trudging on aching, blistered feet. He can't even meet his father's eyes but stares at the ground in shame, determined to say his piece: "Father, I have sinned against heaven and before you. I am no longer worthy to be called your son. Treat me as one of your hired servants" (Luke 15:18–19).

Don't you expect the father to raise a stern eyebrow, give a good reprimand, or at least let the silence settle until the gravity of the situation sinks in? What better way to ensure offenders know the weight of their wrongs? It's *the father's* hard-fought business that suffered the setback. It's *the father's* heart that has been trampled by one of his own children. It's *the father's* right to play righteous judge and jury.

But wonder of wonders, grace appears.

Before the son is even finished speaking, the father frantically motions to the hired help. "Bring my best outfit to replace these rags! My boy needs the family ring on his finger— the one in the jewelry case that I never even let you dust because it's so expensive. And those new shoes I just bought, they'll fit him perfectly. Oh, for goodness' sake, I have a brilliant thought! Remember that prize calf I've been saving for the holidays? Let's roast it today! Invite everyone we know, and keep calling until they agree to come. My son is home. My son is home. My son is home. This is cause for celebration!"

Love waits on the front porch every day with a hand shading his eyes.

Love sees a bedraggled ragamuffin and with a choked voice and tender hug calls him, "Son."

Love runs, not politely and with dignity, but with hair-streaming, elbow-flapping, etiquette-be-hanged urgency, to welcome a wayward child with delight.

And as if deep acceptance, forgiveness, and dash-to-hug-you love are not enough, Grace digs out the streamers, whips up the frosting, and rents the karaoke machine.

Because while Astounding Love welcomes you home with open arms . . .

Grace throws a great big party!

Grace Defined

The Prodigal Son's story is a simple way for finite human minds to define grace. Grace is:

God's boundless favor lavished freely
upon the unworthy and inadequate.

Grace is *favor*: goodness and kindness and more than you deserve wrapped into the prettiest present you've ever seen.

Grace is *immeasurable*, showered over you generously from the Giver of large gifts. No need to get out the measuring cup and catch the dribbles, grace will drown you with its abundance, sweep over you with its vastness, and awe you with its sheer magnitude. Grace is lavishly given in endless supply.

Grace is *free*. Grace does not depend on you earning it in any form. Grace is far too precious to pay for, and frankly, it's an affront to the Giver to even try. Grace is a free gift God delights in giving because of Who He is.

What Grace Is Not

"The Prodigal Son" is a misleading title for this parable. After all, the story begins, "There was a man who had *two* sons." The runaway captures our attention, but a better title might be, "The Tale of Two Sons."

As with the story of Martha, I've long held a secret soft spot for the Other Brother. Maybe I relate to him well since he stayed home and did what was expected: kept up with his chores, rarely complained, and picked up the slack on the family farm when his little brother left. Other Brother was the quintessential good kid living the PDL.

When the Prodigal Son comes home, where is the Other Brother? Right where you'd expect him to be, of course: out in the field doing the work. By the time the Other Brother walks home from the fields, the loud party is in full swing. He hears music and dancing long before he arrives at the house and asks one of the staff, "What's going on?" When the servant tells him his brother has arrived and dad has killed the fattened calf and thrown a huge party, Other Brother is furious—so furious that he throws a silent tantrum and refuses to celebrate his good-for-nothing brother.

The father leaves the party to beg Other Brother to join the festivities, but the son argues,

> Look, these many years I have served you, and I never disobeyed your command, yet you never gave me [so much as] a young goat, that I might celebrate with my friends. But when this son of yours came, who has devoured your property with prostitutes, you killed the fattened calf for him! (Luke 15:29–30)

When I was young and heard this story, I thought, *The boy's got a point. He is the one who stayed with his dad, did all the right things, and worked hard. How come he never got a party?* My tender, little heart hurt with the unfairness of it all.

Jesus wasn't offering a commentary on fairness here, though. He was describing the two kinds of people who need grace desperately: Prodigals and Other Brothers. While Prodigals rebel and try their own way, Other Brothers stay and try their own way. *Prodigals believe what they do can lose God's favor. Other Brothers believe what they do can earn God's favor.*

These two sons, pictures of believers who are a part of God's family, approach the father with their deeds. The Prodigal shuffles to his dad with downcast eyes, hands hidden behind his back, trying to cover his mistakes. The Other Brother strides forward with hopeful eyes, proudly offering his hands full of good deeds and commitment. Though they come from opposite directions, both sons base their worth on the same thing: performance. The Prodigal feels unworthy to be a son because of what he's done, and the Other Brother feels highly acceptable (and wonders why he's not been applauded yet).

We play Prodigal or Other Brother, or a version of each, throughout the course of our lives. We, too, weigh our doing and create post-comma words and a life story based on performance:

Good Girl   Messed-Up   Big Mistake
        Failure   Trying-Hard Christian

We carry that story with us everywhere and especially before God, where we cower in shame or proudly hold up our goodness for a Heavenly Father's approval.

Whether you fashion a "deserving" or "undeserving" story, the fact remains: *true worth can never be defined by what you do.* Your value is based on who you are to the Father. Prodigals and Other Brothers alike desperately need grace to rewrite their self-stories, and these new stories begin with understanding what grace is *not.*

- **Grace is *not* earned or lost through performance.**
Contrary to what Other Brothers hope and Prodigals fear, grace can never be earned or lost. The natural bent of the flesh is to earn its own way. Humans want to be able to do something. We

desire to somehow repay generous gifts. We try to live worthy of grand gestures. That's the way society works, after all, reinforced with phrases like, "There's no such thing as a free lunch." A free gift without strings confuses us, making us duck warily for the catch that must be close behind. But grace would not be grace if we could earn or lose it. Like God's ineffable love, grace is always and forever one hundred percent free.

- **Grace is *not* mere theology.**

Grace was never meant to be just one more piece of theology. The religious and educated among us often try to parse grace, stuff it into a proper box, and shelve it with the commentaries. Even religious leaders often treat grace as just another dusty tome in the Christian library.

Once, my husband Dave sat down with a local pastor. This man leads a megachurch with three campuses, multiple services, and several thousand attendees each week. We'd been attending the church for about six months, and Dave was excited to meet this man and tell him how grace changed everything for us and about the grace-centered work God was birthing in our hearts. Before Dave shared more than three sentences, the pastor interrupted with a disinterested, "You know grace. I know grace. What more do we need to talk about?"

Dave had to grab his chin from the floor when he left the meeting soon after. We were both stunned at the coldness of people, even leaders, who "do grace" for a living without appearing to ever truly grasp it. It seemed that grace to this pastor was just a matter of theology, a word he knew and studied but had never truly experienced.

- **Grace is *not* an add-on.**

Grace cannot be effective when you tack something onto it or simply add it to a what-good-Christians-believe list. True grace is not "plus" anything.

Sadly, many Christian books by respected authors teach "grace + _____." One book I read recently hummed along for ten chapters about how much God loves us and who we are to Him. All of a sudden I tripped over Chapter 11, horrified by the guilt trips that surfaced. There I read about:

- ✓ grace + <u>obeying God.</u>
- ✓ grace + <u>daily surrendering my will.</u>
- ✓ grace + <u>working on my sin.</u>
- ✓ grace + <u>spiritual disciplines.</u>

Yikes! my heart said.

Any time we write something in blank or try to add grace to an overfull, be-godly list, we dilute grace, suggesting it's not enough on its own, and we revert to earning God's favor. But, *nothing you do will make God love you any more or any less than He does right now.* Nothing you add or take away will increase God's favor toward you, and any fixation on doing only perpetuates performance.

- **Grace is *not* a license to sin.**

"Doesn't teaching grace give people a license to sin?" the Romans grilled Paul, the Grace Expert. Paul's hearty response was, "God forbid!" (Romans 6:2 KJV). Grace understood is never an excuse that leads to a life of, "Nah, nah, nah! I'll sin more because I can." When fully grasped, grace cannot be swept aside and forgotten. Grace understood is grace held in awe.

Life is changed from the inside out. Your desires are different. Your attitude is different. Your propensities change. You may have been chief of sinners before, but grace never leaves you as it found you. And grace truly experienced will never become an excuse.

What Grace Is

We only have to look as far as the Gospels to discover what grace is. The Apostle John boldly introduces us to picture-perfect grace in the first chapter of his book: Jesus, "full of grace and truth . . . [while] the law was given through Moses, grace and truth came through Jesus Christ" (John 1:14, 17). Jesus's main mission was to deliver grace and truth and live them in front of us. While Jesus rarely mentioned the word in His teachings, His very life was grace in action. His bold proclamation of why He came sums up what grace is and does in our lives:

> I am come that they might *have life* and that
> they might have it *more abundantly.*
> (John 10:10 KJV)

Jesus offers life. Yes, He offers eternal life in heaven which He guaranteed by His sacrifice on the cross. But beyond a mere "Get out of hell free" card, His invitation is for *life right now*—a summons to enjoy relationship and favor and love and freedom and victory this very moment. Grace isn't just a guarantee that someday you'll be mature and perfect and finally happy in heaven. Grace is for abundant life this minute in the middle of the mundaneness. *Grace is life.*

The Christianity most of us know seldom offers a good definition of "the abundant life." The connotation of "abundance" we know usually refers to money and wealth, and of course good Christians must shy away from accumulating too much of that because of verses like, "You cannot serve God and money" (Matthew 6:24). So, we stay a tad confused about the whole "abundant" thing.

When Jesus spoke of abundance, He meant something deeper and richer than green cash filling an account. The Word Himself chooses words carefully, and when He uses "life" in John 10:10, He means, "Vitality real and genuine, active and vigorous."[6] You could say it's honest-to-goodness sparkling energy in the very act of breathing, walking, talking, and working in this moment.

How would this everyday breathing, walking, talking, and working look? Abundant. An abundance that would "exceed measure, rank, or need in a superior, extraordinary, surpassing, uncommon" way.[7]

Yes, I'd like one extraordinary, uncommon, expectation-exceeding, full-of-vitality life, please! (You want one too?)

Everywhere He went during His earthly ministry, Jesus dished out abundant life like this. He was grace in action, and He showed us how grace adds more life to everyday life.

> Zacchaeus found new purpose and a reason to be cheerfully generous after a "chance" tree encounter.
>
> The woman with the issue of blood discovered a renewed zest for pain-free living thanks to a quick robe tug and some audacious faith.
>
> The twelve apostles' lives were turned upside down so that their passion and significance came no longer from slimy fins but from casting truth and catching real people.

Every time Jesus touched a person's life, He lavished grace all over it, and each person went away with extraordinary help, new vitality, and a story that surpassed common and ordinary in every way.

Jesus wants abundant life for you too. He came to offer you entrance to heaven and extraordinary, out-of-the-ordinary life for the rest of your days on earth. He extends grace for life right now—a grace that makes you come alive.

Overwhelming Benefits

One evening not long after my grace awakening, my husband and I invited Jeff over for dinner. This man is one of those long-lasting friends, the kind you went to college with and coincidentally found yourself living near when you all grew up. Those are fun friends: the ones who knew who you used to be and who you are now too.

The three of us were discussing grace over a casserole (which was nothing out of the ordinary since I seldom stop talking about my favorite topic). I was teasing the two men that I was the first one to "find" grace a few months before. My hubby argued, "I was there too. How can you claim to be first?"

Quick-witted Jeff countered with a sharp look and a little huff. "I got it before both of you. I just didn't get obsessed with it!"

I stared at Jeff for a second, kind of gulped, and excused myself quickly, mumbling about more napkins or something. The comment stung. Obsession's a bad thing, right? But the longer I examined it, the more perfect the word became. When you truly experience grace in all of its fullness and beauty, being overwhelmed and obsessed are natural reactions. Once grace nestles deeply into your heart, your life is radically changed.

Like the people who were transformed by pure grace and truth when they encountered Jesus, you can expect more life in grace—more life in the form of inner security, shining authenticity, blossoming confidence, true acceptance, renewed hope, unbridled joy, permission to explore, resurrected dreams, new possibility, increased faith, bold courage, and deeper passion.

And that's only the beginning! When you embrace and

experience the lavish grace of God, it adds life to your life, transforming your story into something beautiful and desirable.

Grace gives hope. Grace offers freedom. Grace grows faith. Grace rewrites stories. Grace illuminates possibilities.

Grace changes everything.

{5}

A Brand New
Self-Story

After my grace-changes-everything (G.C.E.) moment, a question surfaced. This question that crept in when my belief system crashed to the ground and disintegrated was: "Who am I?"

With the removal of the Pharisee glasses, God had dissolved my very self-definition. I didn't have any post-comma labels left. Before, I was "Janna, proud PDLer for God," but now, "Who am I?" became a scary unknown.

As I waded deeper into grace, God held up a mirror and the two of us stood side-by-side in front of it. For a while I was afraid to look up, petrified of what I would find. I'd just come through the Pharisee debacle after all and didn't know if my tender heart could take another blow.

But when God tilted my chin gently upward and whispered for me to open my eyes, the image in the mirror was not at all what I'd expected. Instead of flyaway hair, uneven ears, a pimple next to my nose, and the chin hair that needed plucking, God showed me what He sees when He looks at me. The picture took my breath away.

To begin to understand the truth about who we are, we must realize:

> Genuine self-knowledge begins by looking at God and noticing how God is looking at us. Grounding our knowing of our self in God's knowing of us anchors us in reality. It also anchors us in God.[8]

How God *Really* Sees You

Do you ever read the short paragraph on the back flap of a book, the one that gives a snippet of the author's life? It usually includes things like where she lives or how long he's been writing and, if you're lucky, something relatable too: "adores dark roast mochas" or "frequently takes long walks on the beach." Have you ever read one of those short bios and felt an instant kinship? Like if the two of you ever met, you'd be instant friends because you're obviously kindred spirits?

Paul, the grace apostle, feels a little like that to me. He's long been one of my heroes and someone I enjoy reading because we adore the same topic so much. When I meet him in person someday I'm going to tell him about the first time I read his bio, post-grace-awakening. Hopefully he'll understand that when I laughed out loud at his impressive, overinflated list, it was because I felt an instant kinship. Paul claimed praise-worthy, post-comma titles like these:

- **Physical**: circumcised exactly as the law required
- **Heritage**: bearer of a top-notch religious pedigree
- **Cultural**: proud member of God's chosen people
- **Occupational**: full-time zealot and law-keeper extraordinaire
- **Religious**: elite Pharisee (i.e., highest religious title except priest)[9]

Here is a man who had everything going for him: pedigree, education, and flawless performance. Then he met Jesus, and his life was turned upside down by grace. Paul grabbed on to the deeper-than-post-comma truth that God revealed, and it changed his life forever. He realized his pre-Jesus, religiously impeccable resume meant squat. He was now a man with a brand new identity—an identity straight from the God of all grace!

Paul writes about this new identity in many of his letters. He emphasizes this subject so much because his own self-image had been so dramatically altered that he never got over it. When your life has been drastically improved, you can't help sharing. And Paul craved that every believer might grasp the truth of a new identity too.

The first half of Ephesians 1 holds one of my favorite new

identity passages. I can imagine an exuberant Paul dictating this letter. Grace is his life theme after all, a grace that transforms undeserving, mislabeled, performance-driven people. Can't you just see him ramping up like an old-fashioned revival preacher, eyes flashing, fist waving, and foot pumping with oodles of redirected zeal?

That's the feeling Ephesians 1:1–9 invokes when we grasp the enormity of what God has done for us in Christ. He has graced us "in Christ with every spiritual blessing" (Ephesians 1:2). Not just a couple, but *every* spiritual blessing! And what comes after that declaration is an awe-inspiring, doubt-defying, glorious definition of you and me.

Oh Precious Believer, by grace through Jesus you are:

Chosen

You are picked, planned for, wanted, set apart as dear, preferred, valued, selected with joy and favor, included, and desired. You are fully known beforehand and still wanted.[10]

Close your eyes for a minute and think about this: the God of creation picked you. He specifically chose *you*. I imagine a heavenly conversation something like:

> You see that girl right there, the one with brown hair and her right ear a little higher than the left? The one with the nose she can flare like a bunny, feet that sometimes smell, and a deep love for re-creating Pinterest pins? I want her to be one of mine. I pick her for my team, to have an amazing

life with me. I love her beyond belief, and I like her. She's extra special to me, and I'd rather have her around than pretty much anyone else!

That's the kind of choosing God did with you. He wants you that much.

In fourth grade my class had a tradition at recess. Each day when the bell rang, we would race outside with one of us holding a large rubber ball. We'd huddle on the asphalt parking lot while the team captains surveyed our motley group and picked teams.

You always knew how the selection would go. First, the best kickers, then the captain's friends, then the fastest runners, and, finally, the rest of us. Boy, that was a nail-biting time. I remember the butterflies in my stomach as names were called. I hoped to be on the team with my friends. I hoped to be on the winning team too. But most of all, I just wanted to be picked. To avoid being the last kid, embarrassed as the team captains rolled their eyes and tried to pawn you off or grudgingly accept you as the pity case.

God is the Ultimate Team Captain. With Him you are picked first every time. He sees your talents and abilities. He created you with them, after all. He knows all about your emotions and your quirks and your tendencies and your dislikes. He's aware of the environment you grew up in, the experiences you've had, the dysfunction in your family (because normal ones don't exist), the happy times, and the sad times too. He knows all of it, smiles in delight, and says, "I choose *her!*"

No last-second decision. No unlucky leftovers. God knew long beforehand who you'd be, and He still picked you. On purpose. To be on His team for the rest of forever.

You are chosen.

Justified

You are a clean, pure, guiltless, whole, no-longer-at-fault, holy and blameless saint!

Maybe you've heard the quick definition of justified: "just as if I'd never sinned." That's not such a bad way to look at this word. You are washed clean. You no longer deserve to be punished for your sinfulness because Jesus has paid the price for you. You used to wear grungy, smelly rags that you tried to make presentable to God, but now, through His Son, you've been given a spotless, white robe to wear, blinding in its brightness. In God's eyes you are holy and blameless.

It was a sunny Saturday in February when I got the call. My pastor from our church in Michigan was on the line, asking me to fly home from graduate school as soon as possible. My dad had just been fired from his ministry leadership position for a moral indiscretion, and my mom needed me.

I flew home to be the strong shoulder for my mom and siblings. Together, we lined a church pew with red faces during the service where my dad publicly apologized before he left for the recovery center.

About four months after the call, I spent a week as a

counselor at our summer church camp. Evie, the young woman involved with my dad, was also at camp the same week. I didn't know she was going to be there. The whole situation struck me as odd, and I didn't quite know what to think. You can imagine the volume of my relieved sigh when Evie and I were assigned to separate cabins.

Unbeknownst to me, God began a great work in Evie's heart during camp, and at the final bonfire service Evie searched me out. With eyes that could not meet mine and a whisper-thin voice, she told me she'd been watching my family the past few months and couldn't believe how well we were holding up through everything. I just blinked and stared at her. Then she asked me to forgive her for what she'd done.

You could've knocked me over with a marshmallow. No words came as I stared at her for a few seconds with thoughts like, "Yikes!" and, "If you only knew," and, "What's happening here?!" fighting for prime real estate in my head.

In that lengthy pause, God doused my heart with what I can only describe as a giant dose of His ineffable love and grace. He gave me His eyes to truly see her, and in awe I realized I could look at this one who'd wounded my family so deeply and tell her I forgave her and loved her. And I meant every word.

Then God picked up my arms and hugged her, and I'll never forget the feeling of holding someone who was trembling so hard she might fall over any second.

In God's eyes, you are no longer who you used to be either. Your sins don't define you; you are accepted and loved.

Instead of staggering underneath a perpetual burden of guilt and being forever tainted by what you've done, you are clean and whole. Today you stand uncondemned and blameless before God.

You are justified.

Adopted

You are privileged, adored, legally His, privy to intimate fellowship, a true heir, and a precious part of God's family. You belong.

As part of being legally brought into God's family, you enjoy all the privileges and rights of a beloved child. No longer an outsider or servant or slave, you've been handed a new name. Now you are gifted with a closer relationship than you ever dared to imagine, the kind of relationship that gives you every right to call God, "Daddy," since you are His precious, cherished child. And you're guaranteed a dazzling inheritance.

A dear lady told me the story of grace-filled adoption in her own family:

I did not know her story when I first met her. She was just one of my aunts and uncles.

Before he came to know the Lord, my grandfather was quite the carouser. I would call him a rooster: he had hens in every hen house. I don't know how many children he fathered, but I do know he fathered my aunt and not with my ever-patient grandmother.

So, this grandfather of mine had this child and apparently her mother was not the motherly type. She didn't really want this little girl at all and wasn't taking care of her. It was very sad.

My grandmother stepped up and said that she would take this child. So she took Ana in when Ana was maybe three or four years old. Knowing full well that it wasn't her biological child, she raised Ana as her own.

By the time I met Ana she was married and expecting a baby of her own, but she was always over at my grandmother's house. She loved my grandmother deeply, and as far as Ana was concerned, that was her mother.

I was always impressed with Ana's story because it showed me what kind of character and tender heart my grandmother had to always treat Ana like one of her own even though Ana was a constant reminder of what kind of husband my grandfather was.

Regardless of your past, your insecurities, your failings or the failings of anyone else in your life, you can enjoy full favor, fellowship, and closeness with your Heavenly Father. He welcomes you as an adored child.

You are adopted.

Righteous
You are ransomed, set free, unfettered, recovered, restored, redeemed, pardoned, pleasing and good. You have a clean slate

now since you've been completely forgiven.

God has made you one of His righteous ones: one who's been bought back from what used to control you (your sinful nature) and forgiven you for all you've done against Him. Before, the two of you had no relationship because your sin stood between you. Now, you and God are reconciled. Your relationship is repaired and restored.

One of the most poignant forgiveness stories I've ever heard involved a young man named Oshea Israel. Oshea was only sixteen the night he went to the adult party, got into an argument, and shot and killed Laramiun Byrd.

Words can hardly describe how Mary Johnson felt the morning she received the news. Laramiun was her only son, after all, and because of this single act she would never see him graduate from college, walk the aisle on his wedding day, or bring home a grandbaby for her to dote on. Hurt, anger, and grief tore at her soul. In Mary's eyes Oshea was an animal who deserved to be caged.

But God had bigger plans for Oshea and Mary—plans that needed a dozen years to play out. Twelve years into Oshea's prison sentence, Mary asked to meet with him. God had touched her soul, and she wanted to reach out to this one who had taken so much from her.

Oshea wasn't keen on the idea at first, but eventually curiosity won, and mother and murderer found themselves staring at each other from opposite sides of the same table. They tentatively began to talk and share their stories.

Then came the moment that left Oshea speechless. At the end of their meeting, Mary looked Oshea in the eye and said, "I forgive you from the bottom of my heart." And she gave him a great big hug.

Today Mary and Oshea not only reside in the same town, but they live in the very same apartment building with their front doors side by side. The two of them share a relationship that looks remarkably like family. He chuckles about her being all up in his business, and she teases him about coming over more often to check on her and take out her garbage.

As Mary puts it, "I have claimed [Oshea] as my spiritual son. It's not pardoning what he did, and it's not [mere] reconciliation. It's true forgiveness."[11]

Despite what's happened to you or where you've been, and no matter how grossly you've messed up your own life or someone else's . . . your mistakes aren't you.

You're no longer defined by stellar or wretched performance. You're fully restored. You're completely forgiven.

You are righteous.

Christ in Me

You are regenerated, new, novel, unheard of, unique, and far different than before. You've been endowed with an entirely new nature, and now God makes His home with you. You have within you a Strength, and a Help that defies human logic. You are released from limits and small expectations, tiny visions, and unfulfilled dreams. This very minute, you have a hidden

Source of Power within you for all you are and do: Christ.

Have you ever experienced a moment when you looked at the circumstances around you and couldn't logically explain how you were coping so well? Those moments are often good examples of Christ in you.

I had one of those moments at the Thanksgiving I've officially dubbed "the holiday from you-know-where." At first glance it seemed like fun: turkey at the in-laws' house, game time together, my sister-in-law travelling in from out of state to show off her shiny, new engagement ring. But about a week before turkey day, the sister cancelled and my mother-in-law succumbed to a bout of vertigo so horrible she couldn't lift her head off of the bathroom floor.

My husband and I considered a quiet holiday on our own but decided to keep our plans with family. The morning after our decision, I woke up with a stomachache as I realized what "holiday with family" now meant: cooking a turkey dinner for thirteen in someone else's kitchen, taking care of mom and grandma (both bedroom-bound), dealing with stressed-out dad, and occupying four nieces and nephews (three of which were under the age of ten). I had hoped for a calm, relaxing day, but Thanksgiving looked a little dicey.

Walking into Mom's house that day was like walking into a convalescent home. The women left standing—me, one sister-in-law, and a tween niece—donned our superhero capes and flew from invalids to kitchen and back. Even the husbands made hero status with their deep-fried turkey. As we mixed green bean casseroles, admired Lego creations with nephews, set out holiday china, took water to sick rooms, and checked the turkey, I was amazed at the continued high energy. Dinner was delicious, if a bit later than normal, and everyone at the table seemed as content as my nephews, who had each scored a giant turkey leg. I take zero credit. It was a simple case of a Power Source not of this world.

Christ in me is the most mind-blowing identity piece of all.

That God makes His home with us . . .

That He offers an endless supply of presence and hope and strength . . .

That you and I have within us the One who created the world and raised people from the dead . . .

This is mind-blowing grace at its finest.

You are Christ in you.

It's All Yours

At the moment you believed in Christ for salvation, God instantly switched your post-comma list for a brand new identity. Your spiritual DNA has changed!

Do you remember Heimlich, the plump, fluorescent green caterpillar from the movie *A Bug's Life*? Heimlich's biggest desire is to be a gorgeous butterfly. He believes, "Someday I will be a beautiful butterfly, and then everything will be better." And you know? He's right.

According to scientific studies, from egg to caterpillar to

chrysalis to final adult butterfly, this animal carries inside of it all the DNA of a beautiful adult butterfly with wings.

Heimlich dreams of the day when his outside self will catch up with what he knows to be true. He ponders and dreams of what it will be like. He's convinced he's on his way to beauty—shiny wings, a slim body, the ability to soar—and can hardly wait. He has faith in what is already true about him even if he doesn't see it yet.

Just like Heimlich, we are on a caterpillar-to-butterfly journey. We are in the process of transforming more and more into what God already says is true about us: we are saints in the image of Christ. At salvation God gave us new "DNA," a dazzling grace identity complete with a brand new nature. And while the metamorphosis process of making the outside match the inside may take longer than we thought, we can still rest in the confidence of what is true of who we are even right now.

"You're telling me I'm actually a gorgeous butterfly with airy translucent wings in brilliant blues and yellows when I feel like a fat, green caterpillar who eats too much, flaps leaves to fake fly, and is often scared of my own shadow?"

Yes. Except I'm not telling you, God is. Second Corinthians 3:18 reminds us, "And we all with unveiled face, beholding the glory of the Lord, are being transformed into the same image from one degree of glory to another." Every day by grace you are morphing further into a "beautiful butterfly" on the outside.

So, what do you do to change into that new image? The PDL-promoters preach at us caterpillars, "Hurry up! Grow faster. Do more. Please God better. Try harder!" But all that preaching only hurts sensitive caterpillar ears. You don't need to concern yourself with changing faster or growing better. The God who created you is the God in charge of your transformation.

Your job is simply to trust that you already possess a brand new identity and to practice living from it. With sheer delight God has bestowed spiritual blessings on you in Christ so you are this person with grace identity DNA.

Today, right this very moment, God says you are:

[*Your Name*],
chosen, justified, adopted,
righteous one, with Christ in me!

(If you want to engage in a little fist-pumping or twerking, that would be entirely appropriate here. Go for it! I don't think anyone's watching.)

God longs for you to know that He sees you as your new identity. Not as a mass of mess-up. Not as a girl who needs to get her act together. Not as someone who should read her Bible and pray more. Not as a pile of boy-that-was-a-lot-to-forgive.

God sees you as His child who delights Him. As a chosen, holy and blameless, forgiven and redeemed, adopted one. As one He insatiably adores and is delighted to dwell with.

He longs for you to know the truth of who you are in your head and then to experience your new identity with your heart. He wants you to revel in the joy of your new identity, to explore it, to grab hold of it, to trust it, to begin to live from its truth. He would positively dance with joy and make up a brand new song about you today if you would take Him at His word!

THNGVB Days Included

My heart always sheds a tear or two for poor Alexander. I kinda want to give the kid a hug, you know, because I know what a *Terrible, Horrible, No Good, Very Bad Day* (THNGVB day) feels like too. I've faced 'em—too many to count. Maybe I never had my foot smushed in an elevator door, but I've been knocked down and held under by a multitude of crazy all in a row. You have too.

I've found that THNGVB days challenge my belief in my new grace identity more than just about anything else. It's when I'm sitting in the middle of a pile of yuck with more being dumped on my head by the next circumstance that I have the hardest time trusting who God says I am.

When my heart is aching and my head is overrun and my mouth is angry, it seems too impossible, too improbable, too unthinkable that I resemble anything close to an adored, chosen, righteous, justified, Christ-in-me daughter of God.

I know you've had your share of THNGVB days too. Even as you've read about grace and shiny, new identity, maybe you've wondered when the other shoe's going to drop. Maybe you've thought, *Yeah, those verses are great, but this all seems a bit too good to be true. I don't know if I have the energy to combat the THNGVB* days. It's been six or seven in a row now—months of those kind of days, I mean.

I get the skepticism. I really do. I've been there with my wheelbarrow full of doubts too.

But, you know what's bigger than our doubts? That truth is true no matter how we feel. Your feelings on the subject cannot change one speck of whether you are chosen, righteous, and all the rest. Truly, they can't! God has bestowed this new identity on you, and your feelings don't change the facts. After all, *feelings aren't truth dictators, they're story indicators.* Our feelings only respond to whatever story is playing on the big screen of our minds at the moment.

Even as I sat down this morning to draft this chapter, I heard the fear voice whisper, *Yeah, but how are you going to be able to say this perfectly? These are deep truths that take years to fully grasp. You're still learning them! You only get one shot in this book to share the depth of grace identity and how this truth can change life forever. Really, Janna? You think you're up to this today?*

My stomach twisted and my heart shuddered a little. The excitement I'd been feeling about my favorite chapter faded— until I heard Poppa's voice, calmly reminding me of what He'd said a mere ten minutes earlier, right before He and I walked upstairs to my office. He said, *I will strengthen thee, I will help thee, I will uphold thee with the right hand of my righteousness.*

My forehead eased, my stomach calmed, and my eyes welled up because He is so right. The old story was that I have to perform perfectly and make sure everything is just right so I know I'm significant and that I matter.

Now there's a new measuring stick: who I am because of grace. And that's what God whispered to me that day. I am His righteousness. I have His help and strength. I can write the words He's planned for me to write because I am who I am in Him. I don't have to worry about being perfect. He chose me to say this right here, right now, and He has not left me alone. He's within me!

No matter what your emotions say or how the voices try to convince you otherwise, the true story is who God says you are. And God's story of you is true on the mountaintop days and the THNGVB days and all the days in between.

The Choice Is Yours

Ira Yates lived in west Texas in the mid-1920s. In a shrewd business deal one day, Ira traded his dry goods store for a large ranch in Pecos County. The ranch was a dream come true since, according to his family, Ira "didn't know beans about groceries" but had a knack for raising cattle.

But the land was unfriendly and the weather fickle, and before long unpaid bills piled deeper than the gulches the ranch hands tried to keep the livestock from. Soon, the mortgage and tax payments were so far behind, threats of foreclosure topped Ira's long list of worries.

In a desperate attempt to save his family and his land, Ira convinced an oil company to drill a test well on his property.

None of the experts expected to find much, but to everyone's surprise, they struck oil. Before long, the almost-bankrupt property was producing a record 8,528 barrels *per hour!*[12]

Can you imagine Ira's delight? How he must have celebrated with tears of joy, remembering the lean meals and worried, whispered conversations of only a few months earlier. I imagine he probably danced around the kitchen, waving the now insignificant bills, a ginormous smile stretching his face.

When did Ira Yates become a millionaire land owner? The day the drilling company struck oil? The day he sold the first barrel? The day he deposited his first million dollars?

No. Ira became a millionaire land owner the day he traded for the ranch, the precise moment the land became his. The fact that he didn't know it yet and didn't live rich never altered what was under his feet. Living hand-to-mouth and worrying about a mortgage payment didn't change the truth that there was oil in them thar' hills!

The same is true for you.

God has given you a brand new, shiny grace identity in Christ. But He lets you choose whether to live as if it's true or not. He lets you decide to step into your new identity and enjoy the joyful, victorious life He intends, or to stay put listening to the well-worn, familiar stories of who you've always thought you are.

Imagine that God stands beside you, holding a full-length, gilt-edged mirror. He gently touches your chin, urging you to look up and see what He sees: an image of you that's better than any you've dared to imagine.

Then God motions for you to stretch out a finger and touch that mirror. If you're brave enough to reach forward, you will find shimmering space where cold glass should be—a space beckoning you to a reality better than the one you've always lived. For the reality beyond the mirror is a place of wonder and possibility. A world you never dreamed existed.

Will you choose to remain in the familiar place? The place that allows you to stay in the Christianity you've always known? The place where you feel comfortable and safe?

Or will you trust what God says is true and step into a reality that alters life forever? *Will you embrace your true identity?*

This new reality will take you away from the comfort of the familiar, challenge what you thought you knew, and lead you on a mind-blowing journey.

The choice of a lifetime is before you.

And if you choose the reality of grace and true identity, there is only one thing you must do . . . .

{6}

The One Thing You Must Do

The end.

I could end the book with that last page: "Only believe." The end.

I marvel that God made things easier than we often try to make them. He said, "Let there be light" and created the world with just some thoughts and a few words. Jesus said, "Come unto me all you who labor and I will give you rest." His "yokes" and "burdens" can hardly be called such because they are ever so light. God's the One who's already accomplished all of the hard things. We are the ones who try to make life harder than it needs to be.

Despite the verses in the Bible that man has tried to twist or put on "Should Do" or "Better Avoid" pedestals, God kept it simple. He planned that the key to salvation and the key to sanctification (maturing into a grown-up Christian) would be identical: *Only believe.*

So simple even a child can do it.

The ONE Thing

True belief is easily misunderstood. Sometimes as Christians we think belief is something we do with our heads, treating it like a Bible study we can finish or something to cross off on the how-to-be-godly list. *Believed God . . . check!*

But belief is an ongoing process, a live-it-now kind of thing. And while belief can be defined intellectually, it will never be lived out only in the mind. Belief cannot be conquered with mere logic. True belief must be experienced and felt deeply in the heart.

We have sometimes been taught that true belief includes something else. Even good Bible studies can leave us feeling that "believe *and* _____" is really where it's at. To be mature Christians we must:

- ✓ Believe God *and* be thankful in all things.
- ✓ Trust Him *and* pray without ceasing.
- ✓ Have faith *and* find God's perfect will.
- ✓ Believe *and* practice the spiritual disciplines.

But this is merely holding on to an antiquated PDL list. When we insist on doing something, we reinforce the old idea that we will feel better if we can prove ourselves. True belief cannot be mixed and diluted with any "must-dos."

Often, the concept of belief seems nebulous to a gotta-see-it-to-believe-it society. We tend to trust what we perceive with our senses, and belief is impossible to see or hear or touch. We have a tough time exchanging what is right in front of our noses for the vague experience of faith, especially when what we perceive in everyday life so often screams the opposite of the belief we're trying to grow. Like the four passengers sharing a compartment one night on a train ride from Paris to Barcelona:

A beautiful young girl is travelling with her sophisticated, elderly grandmother. Across from them is a stately general, accompanied by his devastatingly handsome second lieutenant. The foursome sits in companionable silence as the train enters a long tunnel in the Pyrenees, the mountain range that separates France from Spain.

It is pitch-dark in the tunnel when suddenly the sound of a wet, juicy kiss is heard, followed by a loud, sharp slap. As the train exits the tunnel, the foursome is still silent, each deep in thought.

The young lady tries to hide her blushing cheeks as she thinks, *Goodness, I'm glad my grandmother slapped that handsome lieutenant for kissing me. How forward of him!*

The grandmother narrows her eyes as she fumes, *I can't believe the general would take advantage of my sweet granddaughter like that. Fortunately, she knows how to behave like a lady, and she slapped that old man like he deserved. I wager he'll think twice about a repeat performance when we come to the next tunnel.*

The general rubs the side of his face and ponders, *What an outrage! I've personally taught that whippersnapper aide of mine about respect and discipline, then he does something rash like kiss a young lady he hardly knows. And I get slapped for it by mistake!*

The young lieutenant can scarcely hide a smile as he concludes, *Boy, that was amazing! How often do you get to kiss a pretty girl and slap your boss at the same time?*[13]

Like the people in this story, we perceive what's happening and attempt to create meaning from what we see, hear, feel, and touch. And like the young woman, the grandma, and the general, we often fail to grasp the full truth of what's occurring.

Our perceptions are misguided or limited by a lack of information, and our conclusions can be easily misled.

Seeing the Invisible

But misperceptions are nothing a little grace can't handle. Grace rights our misperceptions, rearranges any untruth we live under, and offers us life as it was meant to be: victorious, intimate, beautiful, and free.

The one thing you must do to unlock this glorious kind of life? *Only believe.*

Believe God tells the truth.
Accept His boundless, ineffable love.
Trust that this beautiful, matchless grace is for you.
Have faith in who God says you are.

"Only believe" means taking what you see in front of your eyes, the doubts you hear in your mind, the voices trying to convince you otherwise, the circumstances that point in the exact opposite direction and affirming, "But God in His grace says . . . ." Basically, true belief means discarding everything you see to the contrary and choosing to trust God.

That doesn't mean the contrary things disappear. Some days the hairy, scary, contrary giants bent on crushing you until you cry "Uncle!" still surround you. Just ask Jairus.

Jairus, a well-known church leader, searches for Jesus one

day. Jesus, as usual, is hard to spot in the enormous crowd, so Jairus determinedly elbows his way through the mayhem. When he finally reaches Jesus, Jairus falls at His feet, and in desperate, heartbreaking tones tells of an only daughter, most precious and adored, who has fallen ill and isn't expected to live through dinner. He begs Jesus, "Come and lay your hands on her, so that she may be made well and live" (Mark 5:23).

Jesus agrees, and I imagine Jairus turning and elbowing through the crowd even faster. "Excuse us! Make way please!" His only daughter's life is at stake; there's no time to waste. But the crowd is fidgety and single-minded in their quest for Jesus's attention too, so the going is slow. And to make matters worse, Jesus is interrupted by another healing that commands His attention.

As Jesus finishes conversing with the woman who stopped Him, Jairus's servants tiptoe forward with teary eyes. "Don't bother Jesus anymore," they tell Jairus. "Your daughter is gone."

But as the hairy, scary specter of death prepares to pummel Jairus, Jesus steps in with a customized belief lesson. Refusing to pay even an ounce of attention to the bad news, Jesus looks Jairus in the eye and calmly commands, "Do not fear, only believe" (Mark 5:36).

In other words, "Don't take what your physical eyes see or what your poor ears hear right now as proof of what's true. Despite how discouraging or hopeless or impossible or contrary the current circumstances appear, just believe!"

True belief is seeing the invisible when everything around you screams the opposite.

True belief is trusting that God tells the truth no matter what.

True belief is clinging to the truth of who God is.

True belief is confident assurance that what God promised is already happening.

True belief is letting God's grace penetrate your heart and secure the victory in the daily battle of seen versus unseen.

Side Benefits of Belief

God longs for you to believe Him. He aches to show you immeasurable displays of His power and desires you to know and experience Him in a big way. Belief lets you see God come alive in your life. It lets you watch God work miracles for you, and it allows you to please God more than you ever have before. These things only happen when you believe.

I became intrigued by the idea of pleasing God when He wrote a new friend into my story just six days after my grace awakening. Natalie and I share similar back stories, and God must've chuckled, knowing the interesting discussions and camaraderie those stories would create. We connected around grace and began a book study together that brought up hard questions as we dove into how this grace life works.

The please-God issue surfaced with a simple question about

a decision. Natalie was feeling guilty that choosing what made her happy might disappoint someone else. Was she selfish (and therefore sinning) to choose what she wanted? Would it please God more to do what the other person expected?

I wrestled with these questions because the reasoning seemed sound to my PDL ears.

- ✓ Selfishness is wrong. Check.
- ✓ We should put others before ourselves. Check.

But what about the pleasing God part? I was stumped wondering if God's happier with us when we deny ourselves, even if it means doing something we're not comfortable with or don't have a heart for. Before grace I thought I pleased Him most when I did things for Him and for others, regardless of how I felt. But grace was showing me that God is far more interested in who I am than what I do. *So, in this newfangled grace life, how do we please Him?* I wondered.

In the middle of swirling thoughts, Poppa shone a light on Hebrews 11:6: "Without faith it is impossible to please Him." The key to pleasing God was not, "Make the perfect choice. Deny yourself. Pick the right way. Obey." Instead, the simple answer was belief.

When we trust God with our hearts and lives and believe what He says about us, His response is, "You've never pleased me more than you are right this minute." Wow. That's so much simpler than the worry-I'm-enough, hope-I-made-the-right-choice, makes-me-tired effort I practiced all those years.

And you know what else? Belief is true obedience. "Only believe" is the best way to obey God. Throughout the book of Romans, Paul gives a clear, logical argument for grace. In the benediction at the end of this letter, he touches on the obedience concept.

> Now to him who is able to strengthen you according to my gospel and the preaching of Jesus Christ, according to the revelation of the mystery that was kept secret for long ages but has now been disclosed and through the prophetic writings has been made known to all nations, according to the command of the eternal God, *to bring about the obedience of faith*—to the only wise God be glory forevermore through Jesus Christ! Amen.
> (Romans 16:25–27)

Paul says, "You know why God bothered with all of this grace I've been logically unpacking for sixteen long chapters? So you'd believe Him! His sole purpose is to woo you to the obedience of faith." Faith in God is obedience to God.

And that's where our PDL stories and any other false stories we hold evaporate. If what God wants is for us to believe, then we never need to fall victim to another "should, better, or must" for the rest of our lives. We need not worry if we're pleasing God enough. He's looking for belief, and He even spelled out what belief looks like: "Now faith is the assurance of things hoped for, the conviction of things not seen" (Hebrews 11:1).

Faith in God is being certain, sure, and inwardly convinced that something is true and real. It's a confident, firm trust that God is who He said He is and that I am who God says I am, even on my THNGVB days. Faith is being so convinced of something, deep down in my heart, that I'll trust my life to it, even when I can't prove it to the naked eye just yet. As Martin Luther describes,

> "Faith is a living, daring confidence in God's grace,
> so sure and certain that a man would stake
> his life on it a thousand times."[14]

Belief How-To

"Boy, Janna, that's a beautiful thought. My heart longs to abide in belief and experience the peace and freedom there, but how in the world do I do that? How do I grow the right kind of faith or enough of it?"

You begin with an easy method, something you've already exercised a dozen times today while you were getting dressed, feeding breakfast to your family, *not* walking the dog, or listening to the radio during your commute: You choose.

No gimmicks, no hidden clauses, no tough puzzles to riddle out. You simply make a choice: "I choose to believe God. I choose to have faith that grace is true. Today I decide to trust that I am who God says I am." And you know what happens when you say yes to one choice? You say no to other options.

You've seen this in action over and over. When you decided to wear the red shirt this morning, you said no to the black one. When you chose to eat the banana, you refused the Grape-Nuts. When you picked the church near your home, you ruled out the one across town. So it is with believing God. When you choose to trust Him, you say no to fear and doubt.

The life of George Mueller fascinates me. As a young man, George decided to believe that we can take God at His word. Shortly after George and his wife married, the two of them sat down in what I imagine was a "We need to talk" moment. The couple determined never to tell anyone of a financial need, even when asked. They vowed to tell God alone and trust Him to provide for their needs.

George Mueller is best known for establishing orphan houses in England during the mid-1800s, when a multitude of homeless children suffered on the streets. Even in his non-profit work, George never asked for a penny. Any broken water heater, outbreak of measles, or unpaid bill was brought before God alone.

And God provided in extraordinary ways: the baker knocked on the door with several loaves of fresh bread on the same morning the pantry went bare, a letter with a few shillings arrived the exact day the rent was due, and the milkman's cart broke down on the doorstep with milk that had to be used before it spoiled, which was enough for every child in the house.

This man who lived and breathed deep faith explains our simple belief choice this way:

Either we trust in God, and in that case we neither trust in ourselves, nor in our fellowmen, not in circumstances, nor in anything besides; or we DO trust in one or more of these, and in that case do NOT trust in God.[15]

The simple choice: only believe.

Belief Growth

Jesus compared faith to one of the tiniest seeds on earth, the mustard seed, and said that even that much faith could move a mountain. Faith starts small, and every time you choose to believe, your faith roots a little deeper and grows a little stronger. You can sprout a fledgling faith faster by feeding it fertilizer, i.e., exercising belief on a regular basis.

Why not strengthen your belief by standing on grace and testing it in real life? That's what I did my first year or so after my grace awakening. I imagined God handing me shiny, new Grace lenses, and I scrutinized anything I'd ever thought or trusted through my new spectacles. Everything from friendships to sermons to food to religious "no-nos" were subject to scrutiny.

Some of my grace friends have performed their own belief tests too. Leslie decided to test grace in an everyday situation. One weekend she headed to a home improvement store to buy wood for a project. She was nervous because she wasn't used to buying building materials and didn't know how to find what she needed. She worried what the store employees would think of her and her project.

But Leslie chose to test out her new identity because she remembered who she really was. Before she walked into the store she gave herself a quick pep talk. "I'm a child of God, and I can do this!"

The employee Leslie met in the lumber department didn't smile much. He grudgingly helped her find the materials, then cut the wood she needed. There was one large piece left over, and Leslie thought it would be helpful to have it cut too. When she asked the employee for a few more cuts, he impatiently agreed, but only if she marked the remaining measurements herself. Leslie asked if she could use his pen, but he gave a short, sarcastic laugh, said he wasn't about to lose his pen to her, and sauntered away.

Instead of being hurt and angered by the response, Leslie laughed inside. The situation was worse than she'd imagined, but she knew the employee's attitude was no reflection on her and her project. She found another pen, made the measurements, had the rest of the wood cut, and left. She never did find anyone particularly cheerful or accommodating to help her, but it didn't matter. When Leslie told me the story later, her shining eyes, big smile, and confident voice were all the proof we needed that she had stronger belief, a renewed sense of self, and more confidence that living from her grace identity actually works.

You can do your own grace testing too. Jump up and down

on grace to see if it holds. Study it up close to make sure it's pure and true. Bang on it with a hammer to see if it scratches or dents. Take it for a test drive in real life. The more you test it, the firmer it holds and the stronger your belief grows.

Belief That Works

So, how will you know your belief is working? What proves belief has migrated from your head to your heart? Why, you will see evidence in your actual life! As my friend Kent Julian says, "What you believe is evidenced by how you live, not by what you say."

True faith is never stationary. Like a bicycle, it only stands up when it's moving. James helpfully points out that "faith, without works is dead, being alone" (James 2:17). Belief manifests itself in action.

That doesn't mean you revert back to striving and performing in order to prove you believe well. Let's not get caught in that devious trap since we have gladly said goodbye to the PDL. Instead, the *natural evidence of true belief is outward action.* When you look down and find yourself water-walking, you know your belief is alive and well!

Author Ken Davis illustrates this truth with one of my favorite stories:

> In college I was asked to deliver a persuasive speech that would convince people to believe a propositional truth.

We would be graded on our creativity, persuasiveness, and ability to drive home a point in a memorable way. The title of my talk was "The Law of the Pendulum." I spent twenty minutes carefully teaching the physical principles that govern a swinging pendulum. I taught that a pendulum can never return to a point higher than the point from which it was released. Because of friction and gravity, a swinging pendulum will fall short of its original position. Each time it swings it creates a shorter arc, until finally it is at rest. This point of rest is called the state of equilibrium, where all forces acting on the pendulum are equal and it ceases to move.

I attached a three-foot string to a child's toy top and thumbtacked it to the top of the blackboard. I pulled the toy to one side and made a mark on the blackboard where I let it go. Each time it swung back I made a new mark. It took only a short time for the top to complete its swinging and come to rest. When I finished the demonstration, the markings on the blackboard proved my thesis.

I then asked how many people in the room believed the law of the pendulum was true. All of my classmates raised their hands, and so did the professor. Believing I had finished my demonstration, he started to walk to the front of the room. In reality, it had just begun.

Hanging from the steel ceiling beams in the middle of the room was a large crude but functional pendulum: 250 pounds of metal weights taped together and tied to four strands of 500-pound-test parachute cord. Sitting against the wall on one end of the room was a table with a chair on top of it. I invited the instructor to climb up on the table and sit in the chair with the back of his head against the cement wall. Then I brought the 250 pounds of metal up to his nose. Holding the huge pendulum just a fraction of an inch from his face, I once again explained the law of the pendulum he had applauded only moments before.

"If the law of the pendulum is true," I said, "then when I release this mass of metal, it will swing across the room and return short of the release point. Your nose and face will be in no danger." After that final restatement of this law, I looked him in the eye and asked, "Sir, do you believe this law is true?"

There was a long pause. Beads of sweat formed on his upper lip, and then weakly he nodded and whispered, "Yes."

I released the pendulum. It made a soft swishing sound as it arced across the room. At the far end of its swing, it paused momentarily and started back. I never saw a man move so fast in my life. The professor literally dived from the table. Deftly stepping around the still-swinging pendulum, I asked the class, "Does he believe in the law of the pendulum?"

The students unanimously answered, "No!"

He believed it intellectually, but he was unwilling to trust his nose to it.[16]

The one thing you must do to access grace is the one thing God wants from you most of all: Only believe! Stand in belief and it will affect your entire life—who you are, what you do, and how you live.

As you watch God work through your belief, you'll see your tiny mustard seed grow until you're overwhelmed at the glorious freedom, unshakeable confidence, and everyday miracles that turn your life into a story you love every single day.

{7}

Life in Grace Land

Twenty-three days after my grace birthday, I journaled:

It's simply amazing to me that since God opened my eyes and started me on this journey, a whole new world has opened to me. Everywhere I turn I find new insight into living the grace-filled abundant, victorious Christian life.

Even as a "little kid" in newfound grace, I was convinced grace was something huge. My heart eyes had opened to the truth that grace continues to change everything.

Grace began to show up everywhere, often in the strangest places. Once I was watching the Hallmark channel and heard a line of dialogue in the middle of a movie that reminded me of a truth about our Heavenly Father's love. I was so overwhelmed I paused the movie for a full fifteen minutes to ponder the grace truth from this unlikely source.

Another time I chose a random fiction book by an author I'd never read and had a couple bleary-eyed mornings in a row because I stayed up past bedtime reading. I couldn't put the book down because of all the grace truth I saw! It wasn't a religious book or a self-help book or anything remotely grace-oriented. It was just grace showing up in unexpected places, like God dropping little grace gems along my path every day.

I continue to enjoy discovering these jewels, examining them, and delighting in their dazzling beauty. And you can too since gemology is simple and delightful when you're wearing brand, new Grace lenses.

New Grace Lenses

When you choose to believe grace, you gain citizenship to a place called Grace Land. One of your first outings as a Grace Dweller is a trip to the optometrist. God exchanges your old glasses—the ones you viewed life with before grace—for a pair of shiny, new Grace lenses. These Grace lenses offer a fresh look at life. Bible passages, relationships, sermons, family, duty, work, play, God, and everything in between are tinted a lovely grace hue. New perspective unfolds before you as you reevaluate your life through the lens of grace.

The simplest way to recognize your brand new Grace lenses and get used to wearing them is by comparing the old glasses with the new.

Love Others Scenario

Old Pharisee glasses: Before I understood grace, I memorized a multitude of Bible verses and filled journals with sermon notes. My Pharisee glasses tinted every Scripture and sermon a murky "do" color. No matter where my eyes landed in the Bible, I found more commands to follow and more ways to try to please God. With my Pharisee glasses on, I felt the need to live up to all of the "dos" I saw in the Bible.

For example, "Love your neighbor as yourself" (Matthew 22:39) meant working hard at selflessly loving others, preferring and deferring to them no matter the cost. My Pharisee glasses tinted this Matthew verse the color of, "You already love yourself too much anyway. Spread a little more of that love toward your fellow man!" And, boy, did I try to love.

One time, with a coworker who was especially difficult, I took the try-hard route of memorizing several "love one another" verses, hoping they would help my attitude and improve my relationship with her. I'll save you the suspense: it didn't work. At all. The only feeling I managed to whip up was mild tolerance.

New Grace lenses: Reading my Bible since grace is a thrill because Scripture is suddenly fresh and new. Several years into Grace Land, I encountered the "love your neighbor verse" again and felt as if I were seeing my first sunset over the Rockies.

When I looked through Grace lenses at the enormity of God's love overwhelming my soul, even on my THNGVB days, and experienced a grace identity that was truly mine, I wondered,

When did "Love your neighbor as yourself" become "Love your neighbor, not yourself"? That thought kept the gears in my head turning for a while, and soon I was intrigued:

> What if God wants you to receive His love before
> you try to offer love? (1 John 4:19)
> What if loving "as yourself" means loving other people
> in a unique way, as only you can?
> What if God knows you need to accept and embrace
> the beautiful piece of art that is you, and then He will
> show you how to love His other unique creations?
> (Psalm 139:13–16)

What a perspective change! With my Grace lenses on, I realized I couldn't fully love my difficult coworker way back when because I hadn't yet fully experienced God's love. I was so busy judging everyone with the old story of "You are what you do" that I was incapable of self-acceptance, much less others-acceptance, at that point in life.

Proper Prayer Scenario

Old Pharisee glasses: With Pharisee glasses, "Pray without ceasing" (1 Thessalonians 5:17) is a mandate for required prayer times and long lists of requests. Bible studies and gatherings promising to help you become a better prayer warrior are plentiful, and the truly godly spend ample time on their knees. Oh, and heaven forbid if you neglect to write down every request at prayer meeting or in a conversation with a church friend. Guilt will hound you relentlessly!

New Grace lenses: With Grace lenses, though, this short verse captures a friendship and intimacy with God that's delightful. Poppa is not expecting you to toddle around on your knees all day with folded hands. He's unconcerned about the length of your written prayer list. And He doesn't keep a heavenly chart, adding smiley stickers each time you achieve extended prayer time.

Grace lenses tint "Pray without ceasing" the color of beautiful fellowship. Poppa is delighted to keep the lines of communication open between the two of you all the time. It's as easy to talk with Him when you're driving or taking a walk as it is during your devotions. And He's just as interested in hearing about the diced tomatoes you're price-comparing as He is your friend's struggle with cancer.

Grace lenses leech the guilt and "should" right out of Scripture and help believers see the truth and beauty of real relationship with a Heavenly Father who adores us. Of course, we still pray. Of course, we still grow into more love for one another. The difference in Grace Land is that in all of our doings, the motivation is different. Who we are matters first, and what we do flows from that place.

So, how's your eyewear? Is there a Scripture passage that needs to be reevaluated? A long-held tradition that deserves a little tweaking? Maybe an old perception or two that could use some fresh scrutiny?

Don your Grace lenses and you'll be surprised and delighted by the new perspectives you encounter.

Benefit of Grace: Freedom

This place called Grace Land is a land of many benefits. Here you are accepted just as you are. Here you pursue the things that bring you joy. Here you are destined to be victorious. This is a land of *freedom, purpose,* and *power.*

Living in Grace Land first benefits you with great freedom. Gone is the need to prove anything since you know you're completely loved and fully accepted for who and where you are this very moment. You know there's nothing you can ever do to make God love you any more or any less than He does right now, and this deep well of love and acceptance frees you from some things.

Freedom From

As you encounter freedom in grace, old things start to fall away. When you live in Grace Land, you are freed from:

- **Old Stories and Labels**

Remember the guilt trips you took so often? Cancelled! Remember those dark days of listening to Shame until you were depressed? Over! Remember the old post-comma labels, those short phrases that didn't fully define you but you held onto anyway? Rewritten! Old voices and stories cannot stand up to the light of grace and the truth of who you are. The further you step into your new identity and listen to God's true story of you, the less the voices of culture, family, religion, guilt and shame can affect you.

Be prepared for the beauty and immensity of your new story to overwhelm you at strange times. At church one Sunday morning, the congregation was singing "In Christ Alone." We'd sung that song many times, but this time when we reached the third stanza, the words bowled me over.

Tears rolled down my face as I realized again how deeply true "no guilt in life" is for me here in Grace Land. I burst into a huge, cheesy grin and had to let everyone else finish the song because the lump in my throat was too big. No old voices or labels can keep us from the freedom of abundant life in grace.

• Old Fears

Grace Land makes Psalm 34:4 a reality: "I sought the Lord and he heard me and delivered me from all my fears" (KJV).

Recently, I saw this radically displayed in my own life. One Wednesday God dropped an exciting four-day business retreat in my lap for a ridiculously affordable price. I had a peaceful heart knowing this event that would help me throw stellar retreats was from Him. By Thursday morning, I'd paid for my ticket, packed my clothes, kissed my husband and doggie, and pointed the car toward Keystone, Colorado.

The first day of the retreat went well. I excitedly took notes about planning and marketing and beamed at the fun new experiences and ideas. However, I detected an undercurrent in the room that I couldn't quite put a finger on. By day two the retreat leader (who'd adamantly promised a safe, accepting environment to further explore our stories and how to serve with authenticity) seemed to have made up her mind about me and began pressuring me during sessions, even calling me unkind names several times in front of the group. By day three the whispered conversations, furtive eyes, and occasional comments from the other seven women in the room made it clear I'd become "The Project." Maybe some people would thrive under all the attention, but I certainly didn't.

I couldn't make sense of what was happening. I would head back to my room after the grueling ten-hour days with a stomachache and a headache, trying to figure out what I was doing wrong. I love learning, and I love retreats, and I couldn't understand the tension I kept experiencing. I shared less and less in the sessions and became very fearful that a giant blind spot somehow hindered me.

By the third night I was so worked up I couldn't sleep. We were scheduled to give presentations the next morning, and I was a bundle of nerves. I implored Poppa, "What's wrong with me? What am I missing? What do I need to change?"

He replied, *There's nothing wrong with you! You are chosen, justified, adopted, and righteous, with Christ in you. None of what you're hearing in that room matters to who you are. You just listen to Me and remember you have My power within you.*

The next day I was able to stand up in that toxic

environment and share my ideas honestly in spite of the "ungrace" permeating the atmosphere. Grace had renewed my courage and rescued me from immobilizing fear.

Walking in Grace Land delivers us from old fears—even deep-seated ones like fear of what people think, fear of being wrong, fear of failure, and fear of not being enough. Can I hear a woohoo?

Freedom To

Usually we think of freedom as an escape from something negative or unwanted, but there's another side to freedom. If I can share a little secret, this is the very best part: *freedom to*. In Grace Land you are freed to more life. You experience more peace, more joy, more contentment, and more of the good God intends for you. Grace frees you to enjoy:

- **Full Authenticity and Confidence**

Life in Grace Land lets the true you emerge. Grace takes the "I'm fine" and other masks you wore to manage people's opinions of you and tosses those false faces into the trash compactor. You're granted permission to live out of who you actually are. For many of us, that means some fun discovery is in order.

Before she was married, Lisa didn't really know what she wanted or liked. Hers was a lovely wedding, but when she planned it, Lisa chose mostly what her parents or her wedding planner told her to choose.

Since grace, though, Lisa has thought a lot about who she is and what she loves. She told me if she were to get married today, the dresses, colors, music, and cake would be completely different because she knows herself so much better now. Grace gave her the freedom to explore and discover her own authenticity.

When you experience full authenticity, true confidence begins to emerge. You become a better decision-maker because you know yourself better. The comments and opinions of others that used to undermine your self-worth no longer phase you. You are more secure and stable in your work, your life, and your relationships.

Imagine being cooped up in a hushed library for days in a row. When you finally walk outside, you throw your arms wide in the sunshine and yell, "So glad to be outta there!" That's how living authentically feels pretty much every single day: happily free to be me.

- **Better Relationships**

As you experience the freedom of more authenticity and confidence, your relationships transform. Living in Grace Land brings more freedom and life to every relationship you experience.

With God: First, the communication line between you and Poppa is revitalized. One of my dear grace friends talks about her God relationship in the most beautiful way. If I ask Candy what her plans are on a random afternoon, she is usually going for a walk with God. She often mentions intimate, practical conversations she's had with Poppa about anything, from what to eat for lunch to where to live. He talks to her, and she talks to Him. She considers Poppa her best and closest friend. Thanks to grace, Candy's relationship with God is open and free, strong, intimate, and meaningful.

With yourself: Grace improves the relationship you have with yourself too. This relationship is vital, because how you view and treat yourself naturally overflows into how you view and treat those around you.

My improved relationship began with being okay with my body. Grace says I'm exactly as God created me, and He never makes a mistake. Girls, do you know how freeing it is to stop obsessing about fixing your body all the time? Oh, I still eat fruits and vegetables and exercise so my body feels good, but I no longer let numbers like weight, clothing size, or age define and control me.

After ditching the numbers, I looked at my wardrobe and realized that most of my clothes worked for former Janna, not grace Janna. I began to explore what I wanted and rediscovered a love for bling, bright colors, and sassy platform shoes. So, I donated a bunch of clothing and embraced a what-sparks-joy shopping style to rebuild a happier closet. The longer you live in Grace Land, the more you're okay with you.

With others: As you mature in grace, you grow comfy in your own skin. Your self-worth solidifies and you are primed for better relationships with others. Whether with colleagues, family, friends, church members, or clients, grace strengthens relationships. You are more secure, so your interactions are healthier. You deal with conflict better (and encounter less of it too). You are more at ease meeting new people. You care better for those close to you, and you wisely incorporate healthy boundaries in your relationships. Since grace I have quit groups, joined new groups, reevaluated friendships, sought out people I wanted to be like, and had more courage in rooms full of strangers than I ever thought possible—all while being a mild introvert!

Grace brings more life and freedom to every relationship in your life.

Benefit of Grace: Purpose

Grace has already given you the "be" of your true identity: chosen, justified, adopted, righteous, with Christ in me. Now in Grace Land, you have the opportunity to discover the "do:" the good work that God prepared for you long before you were born (Ephesians 2:10), the one-of-a-kind thing He designed you to carry into the world, the work He knows you do best in your own, unique way. Your purpose is the thing you're naturally incredible at that also makes your heart sing.

This is where grace meets the everyday in a big way as you explore a life purpose which allows you to engage and serve the world. Grace gives you the permission and the keys to discover the purpose for which you were created and to pursue that purpose into an abundant life of significance.

I once attended a conference where over twenty thousand women of faith gathered from around the world. Several thousand sat in the main location while the rest of us watched a live stream. The atmosphere was electric as the music, lessons, stories, and art gave delightful evidence of God's hand at work in a big way. Hundreds of hours of expert vision and planning had obviously gone into the event.

During one of the final sessions, Jennie, the founder, confessed that over lunch a few weeks earlier she had confided in a close friend, "I have been praying and praying for this conference. But I am struggling because I feel like I am not enough. Someone else could lead this better."

I wondered if any other women in the audience reacted like I did. I glanced around at the immense crowd and the testimony for God that was a direct result of Jennie's vision, prayer, and dedication, and I marveled that no woman—regardless of status, shape, size, or seeming success—is immune to the Shame voice.

Without judgment, Jennie's friend looked her in the eye and offered a grace answer:

"What could God do with a woman
who no longer feared she was enough?"

You know what God could do with a woman like that? *Change the world!* An authentic woman who knows her true identity, has a clear purpose, and trusts God at work in and through her—

that woman infuses the world around her with a life-changing essence. She changes the world simply by being who she was created to be.

The End of Post-Comma Drama

The day God turned an ordinary cleaning moment into life's-never-the-same, holy ground for me, God gave me a beautiful choice. He showed me the two ways to live the Christian life: by what we do in the flesh or by grace and identity in Christ. When I chose grace I caught a glimpse of how grace could craft life into an adventure beyond my wildest dreams.

As I stood in my half-clean bathroom in an infant grace state, gazing upward with hopeful eyes and the beginnings of an everything's-changed world, God whispered one more thing: *This is what you're going to do with your life. I created you to take the truth of grace to the world.*

My eyes welled up all over again, and I plopped down on the edge of the bathtub. In His grace, God showed me my life's purpose right then. It was the sparkly icing on my cupcake, my own little piece of "exceeding abundantly above all I could ask or think" from a Poppa delighted to throw me a party.

Today when someone asks me the question I used to loathe, I beam and my eyes sparkle. The "Who are you and what do you do?" question never bothers me anymore because I know and believe the true story of who I am and what I'm created to do. And I love my beautiful, true, post-comma labels—the ones bestowed on me by a Poppa I adore.

"Who are you?"

"I'm Janna, chosen, justified, adopted, righteous one with
Christ in me."

"What do you do?"

"I'm Janna, Grace and Truth Distributor."

As a Grace and Truth Distributor, I fulfill my God-given
purpose in a multitude of ways. I'm as happy writing a blog post
or brainstorming a new card design as I am hosting a grace
retreat, mentoring, or cooking dinner from scratch. There are
dozens of ways I live my purpose on any given day. And one of
the greatest thrills of Grace Land is that the discovery process
never ceases. There's always more to explore!

Sometimes God whispers a purpose all at once.

Sometimes He places someone in your story to walk beside
you and help you discover it.

Sometimes He dishes out a small piece at a time.

No matter the path, a thrilling adventure follows as you
uncover more of the 1,001 ways you can live your unique
purpose and change the world every single day.

Benefit of Grace: Power

When Jesus told Paul, "My grace is sufficient for you" (2
Corinthians 12:9), He was reminding all believers that the Grace
Land power supply is infinite. It's with you this very moment
and will never falter or run dry. It is this infinite source that

affords courage and strength to overcome doubt and fear, believe the impossible, and live victorious Christianity. Grace is the power at work within you, and it's the power at work on your behalf.

To access this power, you only need to water the belief seed. Your little seed grows as you live your new story, and pretty soon your faith can't help producing some pretty amazing results. You'll see proof of God's power in your everyday life.

Remember the pendulum story when the professor dove off the chair, unwilling to trust his nose to a law he didn't truly believe? Here's how the story ends:

> One of the most fascinating and unexpected outcomes of the lesson was that another student volunteered to sit in the chair. Though he flinched when the [massive] pendulum swung toward his face, he stayed put. Once the students saw the validity of the law demonstrated, they all wanted to do it. The desire to live out demonstrated faith is not only adventurous; it's contagious.[17]

As you believe God more and more, you will see Him work in bigger and bigger ways. Prayers are answered. Dreams become reality. You trust Him more with your life, and your faith blossoms until it can only be called "audacious." Like the brave students in the pendulum situation, soon others can't help but notice the results, and your audacious belief turns contagious.

My mom, sister, and I have a tradition to meet once a year for an annual girls' trip to shop, talk nonstop, watch chick flicks, and eat french fries without exercising. Recently, it was my turn to hostess. About a month before the trip, with sparkling eyes and a breathless voice, I cornered my husband. "I just had a brilliant idea. I'm going to treat the three of us girls to a few days in the mountains. The catch is that I've been saving money but don't have enough for this added expense."

"Well, if you want to do the overnight thing, you better go figure the money out," Dave answered.

My excitement bubble popped as I realized he wasn't going to hand me a blank check like I'd secretly hoped. Deflated, I went on a pity-party walk. As I trudged around the subdivision, I whined, "This isn't fair, Poppa! I've been saving and saving for this girls' trip, and I still don't have what I need to do this fun thing with my mom and sister!" God's quick reply froze my feet to the sidewalk: *Ask Me for what you want.*

I quickly added up what a hotel room and some fun activities would cost, threw in a little extra for shopping (like any smart girl would), and totaled the numbers. He said, *Ask me for that.* So I did. Right there in the middle of the sidewalk, I told Him how much money I wanted and that I was trusting Him because He'd told me to ask. My heart instantly lifted, and I skipped home, confident and excited again.

Over the next few weeks, I was tempted to waver when the money wasn't obvious, but an audacious faith had taken over when God spoke. Soon I smiled knowingly as unusual windfalls arrived: credit card rebates, random eBay income, and an unexpected phone upgrade brought in extra cash. The day before I chauffeured my mom and sister from the airport, I counted the money. Eyes sparkling, I wrote the number on a sticky note with a flourish and did a happy dance around my bedroom. The number on the sticky was the amount I'd asked God for *to the exact penny!*

My delight tripled as the three of us girls enjoyed a mountain retreat and celebrated God's provision together, including a fabulous shopping trip. Sharing the story was almost as much fun as experiencing it.

This Great Power at work in and through you is the very thing that turns life into a grand adventure.

Life Becomes Adventure

As more life expands within and around you, your best life now becomes reality. No more waiting or wondering if it's your turn yet. You have permission and power to begin your adventure story today!

Half of the adventure is learning to love who and where you are this moment. God desires an arm-out-of-the-window life for you. He wants you to enjoy where you are today—to fully embrace each section and stopover of the journey.

The other half of the adventure is dreaming big dreams, allowing your creative mind to ponder what life might look like if you bought the boat, took the mission trip, sold the condo, started the blog, volunteered for the ministry, enrolled in the class, or wrote that book. Given the choice, what kind of adventure story would you love? Guess what. *You have the choice.* An adventure is yours for the taking.

Imagine if your honest answer to "How are you?" was "I love my life!" instead of "Too busy," "Wish I was married," "Hate the boss," or "Getting by."

Imagine if you sent a dinner invitation to the new neighbors and calmly hosted them in your home without worrying if your curtains, housekeeping skills, or food choice were Pinterest-ey enough.

Imagine if during your prayer time you and God took a walk. The two of you chatted about what you love and what you don't. You asked Him questions, and He answered and even told you a joke or two. You laughed together and told Him one back.

Imagine if the volunteer coordinator approached you at church and instead of wanting to run and hide you quickly agreed to volunteer. You are confident in your gifts and desires, and this new opportunity delights you. Besides, you have time and space in your schedule right now since you already refused other opportunities that were not a custom fit for you.

Imagine if after the blasé reaction to your new proposal at work, you whistled on the way home. Sure, that underwhelming response might've spiraled you into a three-day depression before, but not anymore. What others think, especially about you, is their business, and you go about yours with courage and calm.

Imagine if you smiled in the mirror each day because the guilt, shame, and victimhood of the past were banished. Life no longer simply *happens* to you since you've realized you're the hero of your own story. And your heroism is full of grace and the power to overcome in Jesus's name.

Imagine if you opened your journal and reread the entries about that dream you've kept secret for five years now. You whispered to God in belief and heard, *It's time, my dear.* So you took a step. Then another. And another. And watched in awe as God opened doors and formed in reality what you'd hardly dared to scratch on paper.

Imagine if you woke up tomorrow morning with feet itching to hit the floor because you're certain you're fulfilling the purpose you were created for and also adore what you get to do today.

Just imagine if you had your own pocketful of true stories like these! As grace changes everything, these kinds of stories morph from mere imagination to actual possibility before your very eyes. Grand adventure becomes everyday reality. Possibilities blossom before you, offering a new zest for life. Those God-sized dreams you've been afraid to admit are coaxed into the open air so they begin to come true. You are beckoned to carry a unique purpose to a world that desperately needs you. And you discover fulfillment and satisfaction in your beautiful, purpose-filled life.

Of course, a life lived solely in The Shire would become mundane and boring, and life in Grace Land is never just rainbows and unicorns. Where's the "adventure" part of the story, after all, without a little conflict? Adventure suggests you're *going* somewhere and *doing* something. You have a direction, a purpose, an intention. You fight battles and overcome obstacles. You pursue. You engage. You endure. You conquer.

In this grand adventure, your doing naturally flows from your being and leads you to places you never dreamed of, offers you experiences you never expected, and fulfills your wildest longings for significance and purpose. What a ride!

Just the Beginning . . .

"Grace changes everything" is just the beginning, a beginning of happier post-comma labels, friendship with a Poppa who adores you, new lenses, true freedom, deeper purpose, bolder confidence, greater power, and an adventure story that's yours to claim.

Maybe you'll be tempted to fear that the excitement of grace will wear off. For a while I worried that choosing grace for life was a camp decision: the buzz might last a few weeks but one morning I'd wake up and find the enchantment gone. Life would be drab and the sparkle a distant memory.

Now I can personally testify to the preposterousness of that fear! How do you get over something that not only changes your life in an instant but continues to astound you every single day? I've pondered grace for thousands of days in a row now, and its joy, gratitude, and adventure have not deserted me yet. The deeper you delve into its wealth, the more you find how bottomless grace treasures are. Grace changes everything so dramatically that life is never the same. Truly, this is amazing grace.

Like Aslan calls to the faithful Narnians in C. S. Lewis's *The Last Battle*, God beckons us Grace Dwellers, "Further up and further in!" The land stretches before you and the farther you run and the faster you go, the more you discover there is to explore, far more than you could possibly exhaust in a lifetime. Here, every place the sole of your foot treads is yours for the taking. With every battle you face, you are promised the victory. Every dream you imagine is yours to enjoy. Grace for life will never run out or fail or fade because it flows from the God of all grace who will always love you exactly as much as He does this moment. His grace that changes everything stretches before you forever.

So, brave co-journeyer, I leave you with one final wish:

May your heart eyes be opened wide to the
truth of grace in all of its brilliance.
May your tender soul be soaked in the love of a
God who cherishes you so much He sings.
May your true identity permeate and empower
your post-comma everything.
May you choose belief until your life overflows in a
grand adventure story better than any you've read or heard.
And like a little child splashing your toes in the edge of
a boundless sea, may you delight in the length and breadth
and depth and height of the Great Grace you will be
forever thrilled to explore!

Abundant love and grace to you, my friend.

A Note from the Author

Dear Friend,

I imagine you sitting there on your comfy couch, holding this book, and I so wish I could plop down on the next cushion over and chat with you for a bit. I hope that within these pages you have tasted and seen how very much God loves you and *likes* you and how much He longs for you to embrace grace for life. It's my wish for you too.

Thank you for taking a few steps into my story. Maybe as we travelled together you glanced at your own story and wished to experience God's love and grace deeply. Maybe you longed for some more arm-out-of-the-window life. Maybe you whispered a prayer about finding your unique purpose. Or maybe you even wistfully dreamed of taking a step toward your next adventure.

I'd love nothing more than to walk beside you and explore grace and truth together. Won't you join me over at Grace Thread? It's where I ponder new ways to enjoy grace in everyday life and where I write about the thrills and challenges of life in Grace Land.

There you'll have more opportunities to discover what "grace changes everything" means for you and your story. You'll be able to access a lovely collection of freebies, printables, and products that go hand in hand with the book you're holding. You can find out about upcoming retreats and Grace Gatherings. And, best of all, you'll have a chance to rub shoulders with a growing, deepening community of grace-dwellers, excited to live our best adventure stories yet!

Can I save a spot on the couch for you?

Lots of love and grace,

Janna

P.S. Here's a little something I'm dying to share with you . . . .

True I.D. Cards {for free}

These watercolor True I.D. cards are a beautiful way to dwell on the truth of your brand, new grace identity. Download your free printable today!

gracethread.com

Acknowledgments

I've always read book acknowledgments with fascination. As I skim through the names I wonder, *Who are these people?* On snarky days I've even thought, *Can they all be for real?*

Now that I draft a page of my own, I am awed and humbled by the real people with their own stories who have shown up in extraordinary ways in mine.

* * *

To Poppa: For believing in me and guiding me even on the days I felt like a blind dwarf in the stable. I will never get over the awe of being your cherished, chosen, justified, adopted, righteous daughter.

To Alicia: Thank you for remaining convinced I could birth a book and for reminding me often. I love playing our two favorite games—grammar police and world problem solvers—without which this book would be sillier, shorter, and much harder to read. Thank you, too, for reading the fluff and the yuck without laughing too loudly or rolling your eyes. You're my favorite sister forever!

To Carol Tellmann, Marya DeGrow, and the other beta readers: My heart overflows when I think of the grace gift you handed to me. You read the manuscript in its infant form, skimming past grammatical errors and name mistakes, to bravely share your honest thoughts. I am forever grateful.

To Joshua Johnson: Just being in a room with you is like sitting under a refreshing grace fountain. Thanks for being a sounding board and truth teller. Here's to mountain houses, royalty, and grace catching fire!

To Blake: God wrote you into this project in an unusual way, and it's a story I'll never tire of. Your professional eye, "don't worry so much" pep talks, and spot-on editing were exactly what this book – and author – needed. A thousand thanks.

To John Lynch: For being the first voice in my grace story, I hope to give you a hug and a teary-eyed "thank you" in person someday.

To Aaron: For having the courage to recommend a grace talk to me when you didn't know how I'd respond, and for all the "what about --?" grace chats that kept me on my toes . . . love and thanks heaped upon your head.

To Mom and Dad: Thank you for your patience with a PDLer who couldn't even handle the stress of first grade. You shower me with love and a legacy of faith that still astound me.

To Amanda Schuler: God had such fun when He introduced us to each other! He knew you'd be inspiration and encouragement to an author who desperately needed to leave her office to talk to a live person some days. I love our design + God talks.

To Brittney McNeal: Abundant thank yous and a Hobby Lobby gift card for your smiling help during the early research process. I'm still tickled pink by the butterfly expert you found.

To Sarah Garrett: Thank you for explaining the difference between cocoons and chrysalises. I remain fascinated by lepidoptery.

To the dear ministry leaders and Grace Thread followers who granted interviews: I love the way God wove each of you into this process, even turning some of you into new friends. Your wise words and selfless help along the way have been a treasure. Heartfelt thanks for helping me to see what you see.

To Annette, Mary, Friederich, Philip, Brene, Brennan, John, David, Emily, & Joanna: You played a part in my story through the words you courageously shared in your own books. Blessings.

To Dave: How blessed am I to enjoy a best friend, lover, and favorite deep conversationalist all in one? I can't imagine writing the pages of life with anyone else.

Thank you for being a godly husband and a courageous visionary. Thank you for walking this grace journey side by side. Thank you for talking through unformed ideas for endless hours. And thank you for being my biggest cheerleader. You are love and grace in action every day.

And to you, my brave co-journeyer: My heart feels like it might burst when I think of you. Thank you for the precious gift of allowing me to share my grace story with you. Let's dare to dwell in Grace Land together!

Notes

1. Biola University. "John Lynch - Biola University Chapel." Filmed [October 2007]. YouTube video, 31:11. Posted [July 2009]. www.youtube.com/watch?v=7azfoonNqpc&list=FLEbqADbNMu ZiqH3A98i1zlQ&index=14.
2. Oxford Dictionaries, s.v. "ineffable," accessed January 8, 2016, www.oxforddictionaries.com/us/definition/american_english/ ineffable.
3. Taken from *The Furious Longing of God* by Brennan Manning © 2009 Brennan Manning. *The Furious Longing of God* is published by David C Cook. All rights reserved. Used by permission.
4. Ibid.
5. Philip Yancey. *What's So Amazing About Grace?* (Grand Rapids: Zondervan, 1997), 45.
6. Blue Letter Bible, s.v. "G2222 zoe," accessed December 30, 2015, www.blueletterbible.org/lang/Lexicon/Lexicon.cfm?strongs=G22 22&t=KJV.
7. Blue Letter Bible, s.v. "G4053 perissos," accessed December 30, 2015, www.blueletterbible.org/lang/Lexicon/Lexicon.cfm?strongs =G4053&t=KJV.
8. David G. Benner. *The Gift of Being Yourself* (Downers Grove: InterVarsity Press, 2004), 48.
9. See Philippians 3:4-9 for Paul's impressive resume.
10. The grace identity (chosen, justified, adopted, righteous, and Christ in me) definitions were accumulated from a variety of

sources, including *Strong's Concordance*, multiple dictionaries, synonyms, Scripture cross references, and long chats with God. I felt that listing every source might distract from the text and the heart of the message (i.e. footnote overkill). The definitions I've provided are intended as a starting point for believers to dive into how God actually sees them. The true meaning of each God-breathed identity concept deepens in your heart as you allow the Holy Spirit to illuminate and make real to you what God says is already true of you in Christ.

11. Jon Tevlin. "Gunshot took her son, but forgiveness finally came," Star Tribune, last modified April 11, 2009. http://www.startribune.com/jon-tevlin-gunshot-took-her-son-but-forgiveness-finally-came/42833927/?c=y&page=1.

12. See *Handbook of Texas Online*, Julia Cauble Smith, "Yates Oilfield," accessed June 27, 2016, www.tshaonline.org/handbook/online/articles/doy01; and *Handbook of Texas Online*, Lisa Kepner, "Yates, Ira Griffith, Jr.," accessed June 27, 2016, www.tshaonline.org/handbook/online/articles/fyazp.

13. Adapted from "Face Slap on the Train," accessed June 28, 2016, www.nextlevelsalesconsulting.com/sales-insights/motivational-sales-stories/motivational-sales-face-slap.php.

14. Martin Luther. "Preface to Romans," accessed July 15, 2016, www.messiahskingdom.com/resources/The-Gospel/luther-romans.pdf.

15. George Müller, *Answers to Prayer* (Project Gutenberg, 2008), 12.

16. Taken from ***How to Speak to Youth . . . and Keep Them Awake at the Same Time*** by Ken Davis Copyright © 1986, 1996 by Ken Davis. Used by permission of Zondervan. www.zondervan.com.

17. Taken from ***Fully Alive*** by Ken Davis Copyright © 2012 by Ken Davis. Used by permission of Thomas Nelson. www.thomasnelson.com.